MEDIEVAL GERMAN TEXTS IN BILINGUAL EDITIONS • III

HISTORY AS LITERATURE
German World Chronicles of the Thirteenth Century in Verse

MEDIEVAL GERMAN TEXTS IN BILINGUAL EDITIONS • III

HISTORY AS LITERATURE

German World Chronicles of the Thirteenth Century in Verse

Excerpts from:
Rudolf von Ems, *Weltchronik*
The *Christherre-Chronik*
Jans Enikel, *Weltchronik*

Introduction, Translation, and Notes
by R. Graeme Dunphy

Published for TEAMS
(The Consortium for the Teaching
of the Middle Ages)

MEDIEVAL INSTITUTE PUBLICATIONS
Western Michigan University
Kalamazoo, Michigan
2003

The text of the unpublished *Christherre-Chronik* was supplied by Kurt Gärtner, who is preparing an edition in cooperation with Edgar Pape. Their permission to publish this excerpt is gratefully acknowledged.

Library of Congress Cataloging-in-Publication Data

History as literature : German world chronicles of the thirteenth
century in verse / introduction, translation, and notes by R. Graeme
Dunphy.
    p. cm. -- (Medieval German texts in bilingual editions ; 3)
Excerpts in English and Middle High German from the Weltchronik by
Rudolf von Ems, the Christherre-Chronik, and the Weltchronik by Jans
Enikel.
Includes bibliographical references.
  ISBN 1-58044-042-8 (pbk. : alk. paper)
  1. German literature--Middle High German, 1050-1500--Translations into
English. I. Dunphy, R. Graeme. II. Rudolf, von Ems, d. ca. 1254.
Weltchronik. English & German (Middle High German). Selections. III.
Enikel, Jans, 13th cent. Weltchronik. English & German (Middle High
German). Selections. IV. Christherre-Chronik. English & German (Middle
High German). Selections. V. Series.
  PT1384.H57 2003
  831'.2108--dc21

                                2002154634

ISBN 1-58044-042-8 *(paperbound only)*

Printed in the United States of America

Cover design by Linda K. Judy

CONTENTS

INTRODUCTION

The modern reader tends to think of historical writing as a dry, objective form, far removed from the spheres of poetry, imagination and good humor. In the Middle Ages there was no such "Chinese Wall" in the thinking of the learned circles. Fine literature and functional literature overlapped in style and in content, and while some history books, such as the monastic annals, were marked by brevity and sobriety, others could soar to the heights of poetic form, or descend to the most scurrilous levels of bawdy wit. All the qualities which we associate with courtly, pious, or popular writing can also be found in the historical writing of this period. In the fullest sense, history was literature.

But this must not disguise the fact that chronicle writers were serious about their history, and were often very ambitious in what they sought to present. A world chronicle, or universal chronicle, is a history book which begins at the very beginning, with the creation of the world, or perhaps even with the events in Heaven which preceded it, and traces the history of the whole world right up to the date of writing, often with a glance forward toward the end of the world and subsequent events, back in Heaven. Into this already enormous body of material, there is often inserted a description of the world and its peoples, their customs and curiosities. And as the structure of history in Christian thought is profoundly linked to the structure of theology—creation, fall, redemption, eternal life—the whole project is inevitably a religious statement which may be expounded explicitly in lengthy theoretical digressions. A world chronicle is no less than the encyclopædic gathering of the total factual knowledge of the age.

Historical writing began in Germany in the ninth century in the form of annals, but strictly in Latin, and the transition to the vernacular came rather later than in other forms of writing. Latin world chronicles were produced in German monasteries from the eleventh century, and the tradition proliferated with dozens of important works associated with such weighty names as Lampert von Hersfeld, Marianus Scotus (an Irish monk at Fulda), Frutolf von Michelsberg (revised by Ekkehard von Aura), and Otto von Freising. The first attempt at a world chronicle in the German language was arguably the *Annolied* (ca. 1080), which races through world history at a dizzying pace. Its brevity is explained by the way it subverts its historical account to another purpose, a hagiographic one, for which reason there are those who argue the genre question; but it *is* a world history. Sixty years later, the *Kaiserchronik* (mid–twelfth century) became the first German work to have the scale and aspirations of the Latin tradition, though it begins with the founding of Rome and therefore lacks the Old Testament history. Both the *Annolied* and part of the *Kaiserchronik* were included in the first volume of the present series, James Schultz's *Sovereignty and Salvation in the Vernacular*, where they may be studied in more detail.

As we move into the thirteenth century, then, we have a received tradition in Latin, but only the first tentative beginnings in the German language. By the end of that century, three major world chronicles have appeared in Middle High German, one in Middle Low German and one in Middle Dutch. The Low German *Sächsische Weltchronik* stands apart from the others in that it is written in prose; both it and the Middle Dutch *Spiegel historiael* of Jacob van Maerland yield interesting points of comparison. However, our main interest at present lies in the three South German verse chronicles, Rudolf von Ems's *Weltchronik*, the anonymous *Christherre-Chronik*, and the *Weltchronik* of Jans Enikel. These three are close in language, in date, and in conception, yet they also differ significantly, representing the perspectives of three distinct sections of medieval society: courtly, monastic, and urban. They are ostentatious works, affordable only to the highest nobility or the richest circles of the patrician classes, and possession of a manuscript would certainly have been a status symbol. It has been demonstrated that they were intended both to be read and to be listened to; that is, we must imagine them being read aloud to a group of friends who have gathered for this form of entertainment, readers and listeners who have the aspirations to a literate culture but not the academic background required for access to such a culture in Latin. Consequently, these are not scholarly works in the sense that they are intellectually challenging—they were fashioned for a social, not an educational élite.

The first thing that strikes most modern readers approaching these chronicles is their use of verse. The choice of verse for works of serious intent was untypical even in the Middle Ages, though it would not have seemed as strange to readers then as it does today. The Latin chronicles of this period are all in prose, yet in German almost all of the great medieval chronicles are in rhyming couplets. This is true not only of the world chronicles, but also of many early town chronicles and local chronicles, such as the *Gandersheimer Reimchronik* (1216) or Enikel's *Fürstenbuch*, a history of the Viennese ruling houses. This seems to be a particular feature of the early phase of German historical writing. Although the quality of the verse varies considerably, the rhymes are generally purer than they were, say, in the *Annolied* two centuries earlier.

A second aesthetic feature, which unfortunately is not always obvious to the reader of the modern editions, is that these chronicles were illustrated with lavish colored miniatures which comment on the text. It seems likely that all three of the chroniclers in this anthology commissioned cycles of illustrations for their autographs (the original manuscripts in the authors' own hand), and in the manuscript tradition these are copied with the text. The oldest surviving manuscripts were made several decades after the composition of the respective works, but our best witnesses are early enough to give us a good impression of what the original cycles at least of Rudolf and Enikel might have looked like. In the fourteenth-century manuscripts, which are usually vellum, the miniatures are neat, square, framed paintings which fit nicely into the columns of text, but in the fifteenth century, as paper manuscripts become common, the illustrations become larger, sprawling across the page in paler colors. Most early manuscripts were intended to be illustrated, though manuscript illustration was expensive and often we find only spaces where the illustrations were planned but never executed. From the fifteenth century, however, we increasingly find manuscripts in which there are no such gaps, indicating that the idea of art-work had been abandoned altogether. Although the illustration of manuscripts was carried out by a different craftsman after the scribe's work was finished, a scribe would jot down instructions for the illustrator, and these notes can sometimes still be seen in the spaces where planned cycles of miniatures were left incomplete. In this way, the illustration develops from copy to copy in much the same way as the text does, evolving gradually in the early manuscripts, but with a much more complicated history in the later ones, when fourteenth-century compilers made radical incisions into the content of the works. When an early manuscript illustrates a scene, therefore, the probability is high that the original author wanted that scene illustrated, and we may use this as a tool for interpreting the text. Unfortunately, none of the cycles have ever been reproduced in print in their entirety, though the microfiche editions by Ralf Plate and Kurt Gärtner do allow two manuscripts to be studied. The catalogue by the art historian Jörn-Uwe Günther gives an overview. Like the use of verse, the illustration of the text is a major characteristic reflecting the social status of the genre.

Perhaps the most daunting feature of medieval chronicles is their sheer length. Length, of course, is relative. Enikel's *Weltchronik*, for example, comprises just under thirty thousand lines of rhyming verse. To put this in perspective, this is around 170,000 words, which if laid out as prose would fill a little over three hundred pages of a modern academic paperback. Hardly excessive for a comprehensive history book! Nevertheless, by the standards of the *Mittelhochdeutsche Blütezeit*, these were bulky volumes. We might in fact identify as a feature of late Middle High German literary culture the production of longer and longer works by collating and expanding existing ones. The student who thought Wolfram's *Parzival* long will be astonished by the dimensions of the *Rappoltsteiner Parzifal*, a fourteenth-century version of the story which intersperses Wolfram's text with new passages, alternative accounts and supplementary material, quite unperturbed by the fact that in the process certain sequences of the story may be recounted two or three times. Legends, that is, biographies of saints, became legendaries, vast collections of such biographies. And so too with the chronicles: in the thirteenth century they are already characterized by the amassing rather than by the selection of material, and as the tradition develops into the fourteenth century this becomes even more marked. For Enikel was the last author to compose an original world chronicle of any importance in Middle High German, and after him, we move into the compilation phase. This is typified by Heinrich von München, the fourteenth-century author of a *Weltchronik* which mostly consists of sections of the thirteenth-century chronicles and of courtly novels strung together in a loosely chronological arrangement. Nor were Heinrich's the only compilations by any means: most of the manuscript evidence for the thirteenth-century world chronicles must be painstakingly sifted from later reworkings.

For the student approaching the subject for the first time, it is therefore useful to be able to work with sensible selections. The selection in the present volume has been made with a number of aspects in mind. All three of the southern verse chronicles are present in order to allow some comparison of their different styles and milieus. The order, Rudolf–*Christherre-Chronik*–Enikel, is chronological, but also logical in the sense that the *Christherre-Chronik* is a conscious answer to Rudolf, while Enikel might in a sense be thought of as reaction to both of them, or at least to their world views. Enikel is given nearly a half of the volume, partly because his chronicle is the only one that reaches beyond biblical history to give an account of thirteenth-century events, but partly because the piety which Rudolf and the *Christherre-Chronik* obviously share contrasts so nicely with his secularizing approach. The excerpts have been chosen from the beginning of Rudolf's chronicle, the middle of the *Christherre-Chronik* and the end of

Enikel, so that taken together they give something of an impression of the chroniclers' arrangement of material in a continuum from the beginning to the end of history. The four photographic reproductions of miniatures illustrate texts from all three chronicles, representing manuscripts from 1280 till 1430, to give an impression of how the styles of art-work changed.

The texts of Rudolf and Enikel have been taken from the standard critical editions by Gustav Ehrismann (1915) and Philipp Strauch (1891), respectively. Unfortunately there is still no edition of the *Christherre-Chronik*, though excerpts have appeared at various times. However, a team in Trier led by Kurt Gärtner has a critical edition in preparation, and they have kindly released their preliminary text for the present project. This generosity means that it is possible to publish here a passage of the *Christherre-Chronik* that has never before appeared in print. All the extracts are reproduced as they appear in the editions, with the exception of those points in the Enikel at which I have substituted an alternative reading from the critical apparatus (see my notes). The student will notice differences of approach between nineteenth-, twentieth-, and twenty-first-century editors. Strauch has normalized the language of Enikel's chronicle to the classical Middle High German of the *Blütezeit* (1170–1230), marks vowel length with a circumflex (*wâr, zîten*, 13173 f.) and adds a punctuation that is entirely his own. Ehrismann also punctuates, but is slower to change the letters themselves, leaving the impossible forms *wrdin* (159) and *wrtzete* (168) unaltered. Where the manuscript marks Umlaut with a diagonal letter *i*, Ehrismann reproduces this with the nearest modern sign, an acute accent (*ellú*, 4), even when Umlaut is philologically incorrect (*dén*, 19). Other diacritics are also reproduced where Strauch would have eliminated them: *ů, ú, ŏ, ó, n̂*, and *ẏ*. Ehrismann does not mark vowel length, except rarely when it may help the reader to avoid misplacing the accent (*gêstent*, 1554). By contrast with both of these, the Trier group comes closest to a diplomatic printing of the manuscript, and in doing so gives a flavor of the language of the later thirteenth century. Forms and spellings are not normalized apart from the standardization of the letters *i/j* and *u/v*, the capitalization of proper nouns, and so forth. Emendations (editor's corrections when the manuscript is corrupt) are kept to a minimum and placed in italics to make the reader keenly aware of them (7933 ff.). Although modern punctuation is added, the medieval punctuation is also indicated: when the manuscript punctuates in the same way as the editors, this is given in bold print (7980–82); when the manuscript has punctuation where the editors would not have placed it, this is given in the form of raised dots in the middle of the lines (7922, 37). Thus, where nineteenth-century editors sought to purify the work and make it conform to the textual aesthetic of their own time, the basic principle of the most modern edition methods is that the reader should be given as much help as possible, but should also be able to see what the text would look like if no such help were offered.

RUDOLF VON EMS, *WELTCHRONIK*

A highly proficient poet of the second generation of the *Blütezeit* (he flourished 1230–50), Rudolf von Ems, from Hohenems in the Vorarlberg, was a *ministerialis*, a member of the lower nobility working in the service of a greater noble. He is regarded as the most highly educated of all the Middle High German poets, competent in French and Latin and in all spheres of worldly knowledge. Of all the Middle High German chroniclers, he alone earns the accolade of being a distinguished and prolific writer in a variety of forms. Most students meet him first as the author of two courtly novels, *Willehalm von Orlens* and *Alexander*, or of the novella *Der guote Gêrhard*. Also of importance is his legend *Barlaam und Josaphat*, which contains a rebuttal of the concept of courtly love found in Gottfried's *Tristan*.

Rudolf's *Weltchronik* was his most ambitious project, but unfortunately it was never completed. It was commissioned by Conrad IV, who received the title King in 1237, but ruled in his own right only from the death of his father, Emperor Frederick II, in 1250.

> *Das ist der kúnig Chûnrat,*
> *des keisirs kint, der mir hat*
> *geboten und des bete mich*
> *gerûchte biten des das ich*
> *durh in dú mere tihte . . .*   (Rudolf 21663–7)

(This is King Conrad, / the Emperor's son, who has commanded me / and whose request / requires me / to commit this tale to verse for him . . .)

Rudolf laments the fact that Conrad has not received the imperial crown, a question which only arose in 1250, thus the date of the work can be roughly ascertained. The chronicle contains a consecutive account of biblical history from the creation of the world until the time of the Hebrew kings, and the prologue maps out the scale of the original intention, to trace the whole history of the Bible, of the ancient empires and of the medieval world, right up to the poet's own times. Given that the chronicle as we have it stretches to more than 36,000 lines, the finished work, had it been completed, could easily have reached the hundred thousand mark. This makes it by far the fullest of the three chronicles under comparison here. On Rudolf's death, another writer attempted to continue his work, but did not get far: Rudolf's obituary is to be found in the lines 33479–96 (*er starb an Salomone*, "he died while working on Solomon"), though judging by questions of style, his own composition probably ends at 33346.

Rudolf shows great self-awareness as a writer. There is nothing unusual about including a prayer for the poet in a prologue (line 8); that is a set-piece which is also found in the *Christherre-Chronik* and in Enikel. When Rudolf repeats this, however (67), this already places a striking emphasis on the person of the author. But it is the RVODOLF acrostic in the opening lines which is truly Rudolf's signature. It appears also in the prologues to his *Willehalm von Orlens* and *Alexander*, and in the epilogue of *Barlaam und Josaphat*. We might wish to link this with Fig. 1, the miniature in the earliest manuscript (Ehrismann's Wernigerode manuscript, now Munich cgm 8345), which Ehrismann discusses in the introduction to his edition (xvii ff.). It depicts Rudolf dictating his text to a scribe, who is seated at a desk, the manuscript raised before him on a lectern, holding in his hands a quill and a knife, the knife being used as an eraser for scraping out errors. The iconography, a deliberate modification of the evangelist pose, emphasizes the newly established dignity of this genre of vernacular writing. It seems likely that Rudolf's autograph already contained this miniature.

Apart from the focus on the author, Rudolf's prologue follows conventional patterns. An *invocatio* (1–28) is followed by a spiritual meditation (29–60), both of which focus on God's act of creation, since this will be the starting point of the work itself (189 ff.). Then comes a prayer for the poet and his work (61–74) which spills over into a statement of intent, a summary of the pattern of history which will be the structure of the whole chronicle: first a brief outline of sacred history (75–146), then of secular history (147–88). The six "worlds" into which Rudolf divides sacred history here are the *sex aetates mundi* (six ages of the world; singular: *aetas*) which were first worked out as a historiographical schema by Augustine, and which were by far the most popular pattern in historical writing in the Middle Ages:

1. Adam to Noah
2. Noah to Abraham
3. Abraham to David
4. David to the Babylonian Captivity
5. Babylonian Captivity to Christ
6. Christ to the Second Coming

These are Rudolf's main structuring principle, as they are for many medieval world chronicles, and he marks the beginning of each age with an

Figure 1. The author dictates his work to a scribe. Rudolf von Ems, *Weltchronik* (fol. 1r). Munich, Bayerische Staatsbibliothek: cgm 8345, vellum, ca. 1270–80.

acrostic, NOE (867), ABRAHAM (3794), etc. In the prologue he follows Augustine's divisions precisely, but in the body of the chronicle he varies the scheme, whether by design or by error, in that he has the fourth *aetas* begin with Moses (8798) and the fifth with David (21518); presumably he would have to have compensated by omitting the division at the Babylonian Captivity, but of course his chronicle breaks off before this point is reached.

Rudolf's verse style is far more sophisticated than that of Enikel or the *Christherre*-poet. His vocabulary is varied, his imagery works well, and (in contrast to Enikel) his rhymes are effortless. He makes a feature of the repetition of a word across the two lines of a couplet, the same lexical choice being used with differing forms, functions or meanings within tight syntactic units, which makes the prologue extremely difficult to translate. We might note the coupling of synonyms in lines like 279, or the frequent use of lists. Often the sentences become very long, with apparently endless strings of relative clauses usually producing a very fine flowing style; only rarely, as in 339 ff., does the grammatical reference appear to go missing. Of course, whether a pronoun is a relative or a demonstrative is often a question of punctuation, so that it is entirely a matter of interpretation whether a new sentence begins, say, in 19, 135, or 228. We are certainly not obliged to agree with Ehrismann.

When recounting biblical history, Rudolf has, as one might expect, a fairly conservative approach to his source, and seldom alters details. His principal source is the twelfth-century *Historia scholastica* of Peter Comestor, a handbook to the Bible which by the thirteenth century was already immensely popular. It gave a complete retelling of all Old Testament history with exegetical comments and explanations, additional narrative details from popular and Jewish traditions, and inserted material on parallel events in non-biblical ancient history. Rudolf is also working with a Vulgate (Latin Bible), which he mentions in 183, but the Comestor is certainly his source for much of his material, including the *sex aetates*. Rudolf's creation of the world follows Genesis 1 closely, but as we move into the geography of paradise and the story of the fall (253 ff.), which ultimately derive from Genesis 2 and 3, a number of details appear that betray the influence of the *Historia scholastica*. The story of the biblical protoplasts, Adam and Eve, is particularly important for the medieval world-view. Adam was believed literally to be our first forefather, his sin was the origin of all evil and suffering, and his foreshadowing of Christ (the "new Adam" of 1 Corinthians 15.22, 45) put him in the center of Christian theology. Allusions to Adam and Eve were everywhere in medieval art and literature. In this very important passage, Rudolf sets the standards for his biblical narrative: though he remains close to the Vulgate, he very obviously shows the Comestor's influence. For example, the devil (345) is not mentioned in the Genesis stories, but features largely in the Comestor's commentary. On the other hand, the detail for which the Comestor's Adam narrative is most famous, that the serpent had a female face, is not repeated here. Deviations from the source do occur. If line 350 implies an infernal council (see my note), the idea is drawn from general knowledge of the Adam stories, not from the Comestor. Or again, it is interesting that Rudolf has transferred the "protevangelical verse" (Gen. 3.15), presumably by mistake: the Bible speaks of how the "seed" of the woman will bruise the head of the serpent, which Christian exegesis takes as a prophecy of Christ defeating the devil, but Rudolf makes it Eve herself who will strike the devil, inviting perhaps an

interpretation related to Mary (397). An analysis of this sort, looking at the
origins and significance of deviations from the Bible, is a useful approach
to the biblical narrative in all the chronicles.

Following the Latin tradition of combining universal history with geographical writing, Rudolf switches after his account of the Tower of Babel
to a survey of the wonders of the three continents (1353–3088). This, of
course, is almost the point at which the Bible has the "Table of Nations"
(Genesis 10). Noah's family have begun to repopulate the world after the
flood, his three sons become the progenitors of 72 tribes who spread out
across the continents, the aetiological story of Babel explains the scattering
of languages, and thus the nations are born; this is the natural point at
which to list them. It is interesting that Enikel also associates his very much
shorter geographical survey with Babel (27357–652), even though he places
it toward the end of his chronicle and has already had the Babel story itself
with a short list of nations at its proper place (3245–424). Rudolf's 1700-
line geography is, however, not based on the table in Genesis, but rather is
derived from the first book of the *Imago mundi* of Honorius Augustodunensis, an early twelfth-century reference book on geography, physics,
astronomy and chronology, which also includes a survey of world history in
its third book. Like Honorius, Rudolf begins with a description of Asia,
then Europe (2181) and finally Africa (2759). On the relatively familiar
geography of Europe he focuses especially on Germany, Denmark, Greece,
and Britain, and a series of German-speaking cities are described in some
detail: Constance, Basel, Strasbourg, Speyer, Worms, Mainz, and Cologne,
with many important details of contemporary life. But the descriptions of
the unfamiliar continents, Asia and Africa, are possibly even more interesting. Our extract is from the description of India, in which Rudolf deals
first with Indian "races" (1491–1668), then with monsters and beasts
(1669–1799). It follows closely Honorius's chapters 10 (on peoples of
India), 11 (on monsters), and 12 (on fabulous beasts), and shows well the
mixture of fact and fantasy which made up the medieval perception of the
world beyond Europe. The data on the Brahmans (1533) show that Medieval
Europe did have more information on eastern religions than we often
imagine, but the accounts of monsters, which were recorded in all serious-
ness and literally believed, sound to us like the wildest sort of travellers'
tale. In medieval thinking, the "monstrous races," which are in some sense
human, are to be strictly distinguished from "monsters" or fabulous beasts,
but both have the same theological function, to contrast the wholeness of
the Christian world with the imperfection of "heathendom" and realms
beyond. Ultimately this large body of detailed information goes back to lists
in the geography books of the classical author Pliny, known in the Middle
Ages mainly through an epitome by Solinus. Some are even older, such as

the Pygmies, who originate in Homer. Many of the names which turn up in medieval texts as exotic races of the east apparently belonged to real peoples in Roman times. Thus, the Orestae were originally a people of Macedonia, the Choatrae of Scythia. The Garamantes are listed by Pliny as an exotic people in Ethiopia who do not marry; in lists of monstrous peoples, India and Ethiopia are often conflated, and in such maps as the Hereford *Mappa mundi*, Rudolf's "Indian" races are bunched together in North Africa. Like-wise, some of the fantastic beasts may contain rudiments of fact. The unicorn, for example, may have arisen from travellers' reports of sightings of rhinoceroses; in Latin texts, *unicornuus* (or *monoceros*) and *rhinoceros* are sometimes distinguished, sometimes conflated. In the course of the Middle Ages, this body of lore grew to considerable proportions. We can see this operating in the case of the giant Pandae (Macrobii), who originally had the peculiarity of being born grey-haired. Later, however, this attribute was separated off and given to a different race, to increase the number of races in the catalogue, and hence they appear separately also in Rudolf's list (1525; 1590). Rudolf is concerned to make his description convincing, and expands the source greatly. For example, verses 1491–95 are based on just four words in Honorius: *India habet xliiii regiones* (India has 44 provinces). And yet, he adds very little hard content of his own. The expansion is a question of poetry and padding, transforming Honorius's telegramatic style into a text with a literary niveau.

When reading Rudolf's prologue or biblical narrative, one has the impression of a writer of some piety. The overall tone of such passages reflects the Comestor's influence almost as much as the actual details do. Obviously, Rudolf had enjoyed the sound basic theological education which was a standard part of all medieval schooling, but he was not a theologian, and none of his works show any great interest in the theological contro-versies of the thirteenth century. Despite the respect for religion which resounds through the biblical narratives, Rudolf was a courtly, not a monastic writer. The difference is less obvious in the creation-fall narrative, but once he reaches the intrigues of later biblical history, the mindset of courtly literature clearly affects his presentation of events. This is what Horst Wenzel has called *Höfische Geschichte*: the language and categories of courtly culture shine through in the presentation of history. We may find elements of *minne*, for example in the story of David and Bathsheba, and of *aventiure* in the battle scenes. We do not know how Rudolf would have handled post-biblical history, but we might guess that his approach there would be even more like that in his courtly novels.

The sphere in which the courtly Rudolf really shines through is in everything which pertains to secular kingship. In his prologue he is at pains to say that he is interested in presenting both *Heilsgeschichte* and *Weltge-schichte*. The prologue in fact traces the whole of history first with the focus on sacred history, and then a second time with the focus on the secular world, a procedure which is reminiscent of the *Annolied*, though there is no evidence that Rudolf intended like the *Annolied* poet to structure his whole chronicle in this way. It would have been fascinating to see him put his program into practice in a history of the medieval emperors, but alas the chronicle never reaches this point. But we do get a foretaste of it in his account of the royal house of Israel. The relative length of this section of the chronicle is already an indicator of its importance. And here, right after the DAVID acrostic marking the beginning of the fifth age, Rudolf brings us an elegy in praise of the patron of the work, Conrad IV (21518–740). *David rex et propheta* was seen as foreshadowing all Christian kingship, and here he is brought into direct association with Conrad, who, like David, was also King of Jerusalem. In the same passage we find criticism of those who opposed his election, for Conrad never did wear the imperial crown (21610). Since the main opposition to the Hohenstaufen came from the papacy, the political struggles of the period were in large part a question of the relationship between *sacerdotium* and *imperium*. If Helmut Brackert's interpretation is correct, Rudolf has already touched on this theme: when in his geographical survey he reaches Rome, he deviates from his source to note that the throne in this city has spiritual authority—by implication, only spiritual. We may conclude, then, that Rudolf's entire historical construction serves the purpose of Hohenstaufen legitimation. The early parts of the chronicle lead up to the Hebrew kings; this kingdom is brought into association with contemporary kingship and then recounted at great lengths. In all probability, the age of David would itself have been a springboard to even longer accounts of the great empires of Alexander (which, we remember, is the theme of another work by Rudolf), of Rome, and of the Christian world, culminating in the lives of the Hohenstaufen dynasty. It is in this overall plan that the courtly perspective most clearly shines through as the determining factor in Rudolf's *Weltchronik*.

CHRISTHERRE-CHRONIK

Rudolf opened his chronicle with the lines:

> *Richter Got, herre ubir alle kraft.*
> *Vogt himilschir herschaft . . .*   (Rudolf 1 f.)

Only a few years later, a second verse world chronicle was composed in Middle High German, starting with the very similar lines:

> *Crist herre keiser uber alle craft*
> *Voit himelischer herschaft . . .*   (*Christherre-Chronik* 1 f.)

In stark contrast to Rudolf's bold proclamation of his own authorship, this chronicle gives no clue as to the identity of the poet, and is known instead by its opening words, the *Christherre-Chronik*. The only solid information we have about its origins is found in a dedication in the prologue, which shows similarities in formulation to Rudolf's dedication:

> *Des gebot mich des gebetin hat*
> *Daz dran erbeite mich*
> *Min here lantgreue Heinrich*
> *Von Duringen der uurste wert*
> *Der des hat an mir gegert*
> *Daz ich daz buch berichte*
> *Von latin in duisch geiichie . . .*   (*Christherre-Chronik* 278–84)

(His command requested of me / that I exert myself on this task, / my Lord, Landgraf Heinrich / von Thüringen, the worthy prince, / who desired of me / that I should prepare this book, / translating it from Latin into German verse . . .)

The commissioner of the work, then, was Heinrich der Erlauchte of Thuringia, whose reign (1247–88) provides the main parameters for dating the work. Inter-textual considerations mean that it must have been written after Rudolf's chronicle, so we tend to think of the later 1250s or the 1260s as the date of composition, though it could be later, and there is no absolute guarantee for the usual assumption that it predates Enikel. These same verses also clarify the geographical provenance, hence older scholarship sometimes refers to the *Thüringische Weltchronik*. Style and interests strongly suggest a monastic writer. Anything beyond this is speculation. Like Rudolf, the *Christherre*-poet never completed his work. It breaks off even earlier, with Adoni-Bezek in the first chapter of the Book of Judges, after just 24,330 lines, and in the earliest compilations, Rudolf's narrative from Judges to Kings is used as a first *continuatio*.

The monastic setting is of course a hypothesis, but there is a precedent for it. The *Kaiserchronik*, written in Regensburg some 120 years earlier, is also thought of as the work of a monastic writer with a secular patron. This comparison is interesting, as the *Kaiserchronik* and the *Christherre-Chronik* do to some extent share a perspective which is absent from the secular chronicles. Both focus on salvation history with an obvious element of preaching in the presentation. Both have some systematic theological reflection, the *Christherre-Chronik* in its unusually long prologue, the *Kaiserchronik* in its disputations. One can imagine both of these works being written in a monastic library, the poet surrounded by the whole tradition of Christian piety, and their common aim is to present these truths to the courtly world; if they had been writing for their own monastic community, of course, monks would have written in Latin. Yet ironically, the anecdotal style of the *Kaiserchronik* and the flexible way it handles its sources are more like Enikel, the most secular of all our chronicles. The reason for this would seem to be that the *Kaiserchronik* begins with the foundation of Rome, avoiding biblical history and focusing on the conversion of the Empire, whereas the *Christ-herre-Chronik* contains only Old Testament narrative, which the monastic writer must handle with particular reverence.

The relationship of the *Christherre-Chronik* to Rudolf's *Weltchronik* raises interesting questions on the divisions of medieval society. The similarity of the opening couplets led nineteenth-century scholarship to the opinion that this was nothing but a corrupt text of Rudolf. In fact, the two have little more than this couplet in common. There are many places where similar-ities of wording might suggest that the later poet has an eye on the earlier: in our excerpt, compare lines 8057 f. with Rudolf's *durh ir liebe unz uf das zil: / des duhtin durh si niht ze vil* (6186 f.). But these are more echoes than cita-tions, and may even be coincidental. Nevertheless, the parallel opening can hardly be a coincidence, and the modern consensus is that the later poet knew Rudolf, though he was not using him as a direct source. If the *Christ-herre*-poet is not wishing to imitate Rudolf, as much twentieth-century schol-arship assumed, then, as current theory would have it, he must be seeking consciously to distance himself from his predecessor. As we have seen, Rudolf's courtly perspective shines through in his emphasis on secular his-tory, in his pursuit of all branches of knowledge, in narrative elements of courtly culture, and in his interest in the theory of kingship. None of this is present in the *Christherre-Chronik*, which sticks mostly to biblical narrative, follows its sources closely and focuses on theological perspectives. The pro-logue demonstrates the interest in systematic theology which is notably absent in Rudolf. The overall plan is very similar to Rudolf's, to chart the history of the six ages, using the Vulgate and the *Historia scholastica* as the principal sources, but here with the deliberate exclusion of any but a brief passing excursion into worldly matters. One important difference between Rudolf and the *Christherre-Chronik* is the latter's lack of a geographical sec-tion: a brief reference at the point where Rudolf places his table of nations shows that the poet is familiar with this idea but chooses not to make too much of it. It seems likely that we have in this work a conscious attempt to repeat the earlier project with a different emphasis. Monika Schwabbauer has brought this down to a simple contrast: Rudolf is writing *Weltgeschichts-dichtung*, the anonymous *Christherre*-poet, *Bibeldichtung*.

Figure 2. Theophany at Bethel: Jacob's dream of the ladder. Compilation: *Christherre-Chronik*, with excerpts of Jans Enikel, *Weltchronik* (fol. 48rb). Munich, Bayerische Staatsbibliothek: cgm 5, vellum, ca. 1370.

Our excerpt comes from the latter part of the book of Genesis, but taken from the Comestor, as a series of smaller details reveals. It follows the source pedantically. If the story of Jacob's wedding is entertaining, this is not because the poet has made it so, but because it is already entertaining in the Bible. The chronicle's only innovation here is an occasional typological interpretation which goes beyond what was found in the *Historia scholastica* (7951 ff.). One might consider whether the hint that the moonshine was dull on Jacob's wedding night is an attempt to make his naïveté less reprehensible (8094); anyone reading this story must wonder how Jacob could fail to notice that the young women have been switched, and some medieval versions of the story, such as Enikel's, offer very elaborate mitigating circumstances. In a very modest way, the *Christherre*-poet may be making a similar concession. On the other hand, the element of love is not played up much more than it is in the sources. This is one of the passages where Rudolf allowed himself unmistakably to be influenced by the *minne* cult. The *Christhere-Chronik* also has some of the key terminology of courtly love in this text: *nach wunsche wol getan* (8025), *minne* (8068), *dienst* (8070); but the Bible's *Rahel decora facie et venusto aspectu quam diligens Iacob* ("Rachel was fair of face and of pleasant appearance, and Jacob loved her," Gen. 29.17 f.) must be translated somehow, and the focus of *dienst* is Jacob's servant status in Laban's house rather than *minnedienst* in an abstract sense. A full study of courtly elements in this chronicle has never been attempted, but they are certainly less prominent than in Rudolf.

In the middle of the excerpt we find a good example of an *incidens* (plural: *incidentia*). This is a short insert into the account of sacred history with information about what was going on in "heathen" history at the time. The Comestor invented the term and provided the model for subsequent writers, among them Gottfried of Viterbo, who used them in his *Pantheon*, a Latin world chronicle. Both Rudolf and the *Christherre-Chronik* have a series of *incidentia*, and as the Comestor is in any case their major source of biblical narrative, it has often been stated that he is the source for these, too. In fact, however, only one of the *incidentia* in the *Christherre-Chronik*—the one in our excerpt—is taken from the Comestor, Gottfried's *Pantheon* being the source for the rest. This tenth *incidens* is based on the Comestor's fifth *incidens*. The opening line (8231) indicates a separate parallel narrative, as we hear briefly what was happening in Greece during the lifetime of Jacob. The monastic writer is less interested in the Greek kings than in the person of Minerva. A recurrent problem for medieval historians was what to make of the ancient deities who crop up in otherwise authoritative sources. The simple solution is to present them as mortals and lament the folly of those who have taken them to be divine.

JANS ENIKEL, *WELTCHRONIK*

"Enikel" is not a name; it is in fact nothing more than one of the medieval forms of the word *Enkel*. The poet was called Jans; he was named after his grandfather, and was therefore *Jans, der Jansen enikel*. When we refer to "Enikel" as though this were a surname, we are in fact perpetuating a seventeenth-century error, but it has become a handy convention, and we stick with it. Jans Enikel was a member of the Viennese patrician élite, one of the first representatives of a new literary world which was emerging in the thirteenth century—the town. His second literary project, the *Fürstenbuch*, is in fact the earliest attempt at a history of the city of Vienna, which apparently he almost completed: it breaks off about the time of his own childhood. However, the choice of a world chronicle for his first and most important work is very significant. This form is ideal for any writer seeking new patterns in history, and just as Rudolf used it to undergird the manifest destiny of the Hohenstaufen, just as the *Annolied* uses it to place Anno II of Cologne in the center of history and Otto von Freising to strengthen the position of his nephew Frederick I (Barbarossa), so Enikel saw here the opportunity to give urban society a sense of its own historical identity.

Various records of the Viennese patriciate document the life of a Jans who is in all probability our chronicler. If this identification is correct, he is one of the best attested Middle High German writers: his family tree, his connections, his father's position as *Stadtrichter*, his mother's residence in a convent, his children, even his street address in Vienna, are recorded. From about 1275 he is known in the town as Herr Johannes der Schreiber, which tallies with an indication in the *Weltchronik* that it, or at least the papal catalogue which it contains after line 22284, was written in 1272: there we are told that Gregory X (1271–76) has been Pope for one year. Nevertheless, there are still those who would argue for a far later date of writing, even after 1288, on the basis of source hypotheses. Perhaps a distinction should be made between the dates of the first and second versions, for it seems Enikel made at least two. The standard text is based on MSS 1 (Munich) and 2 (Regensburg), but the important MSS 9 (Leipzig) and 10 (Berlin) often have the best readings which we may think of as Enikel's corrections, and they seem to contain later additions by the original author. In our excerpt, a few verses from MS 10 have been included after lines 28074 and 28078.

The overall shape of Enikel's chronicle parallels that of Rudolf and the *Christherre-Chronik*, except that the *aetas* doctrine, to which he twice pays lip-service, is never developed. He begins with a re-telling of Old Testament history, goes over to the tales of the Trojan war and of Alexander, then turns to Rome and follows the succession of Emperors right up to his own time, occasionally skipping whole centuries, but giving extensive coverage to his favorite characters, especially Charles the Great and Frederick II. The style is anecdotal, with a large proportion of direct speech. To some extent this is modelled by the *Kaiserchronik*, which is also a source for part of the material on emperors, but whereas the tales and legends of the *Kaiserchronik* serve as moralizing exempla, Enikel's are often more reminiscent of the *Schwank*, with its scurrilous, bawdy humor. Frequent prose inserts such as that after line 28690 in our excerpt add such factual data as dates, or serve as headings, especially in MS 9. The narrative is interrupted towards the end for a number of more cataloguing sections. The list of popes which has been mentioned in connection with dating is simply a table of names with the lengths of their pontificates. The description of the customs of the Germans and their European neighbors, which we have compared to the geographical surveys in other chronicles, is in verse, but the section on German kings and on the genealogy of the Babenberg Dukes of Austria is in prose. The question of Enikel's sources is far more difficult than with Rudolf and the *Christherre-Chronik*, for he appears to be using a wider variety of materials, which he conflates and adapts at will, and he seems also to draw on oral tradition. Clearly he did not share his predecessors' reverence for the authority of a Latin text. The much-cited opinion that Honorius's *Imago mundi* was his major source has been discredited.

The most distinctive feature of Enikel's *Weltchronik* is its presentation of urban perspectives. Old Testament characters appear as merchants defending their trading interests; Abraham's tent becomes a townhouse with an inner courtyard. Cynical aphorisms reflect the canny instinct of the businessman: a penny is worth two halfpennies—if they're real (26547). Courtly elements are also to be found, partly because the new urban literary culture took courtly literature as its model, partly because the patrician élite themselves had pretensions to a kind of nobility. But in contrast to Rudolf, Enikel's *minne* quickly degenerates to something far less pure. A good example of this is the story of the knight who jousts in his lady's chemise. This is based on an Old French tale which is firmly in the courtly tradition, but Enikel turns it from a test of true love into a manipulative sexual power struggle. Where the earlier chronicles idealistically espoused courtliness or piety, Enikel is far less ideological. Sometimes one has the impression he is simply using the world chronicle as a framework within which to entertain us with a series of memorable stories. But he does have a program, and this comes out most clearly when he attacks the traditional interpretation of the Ham story by which the medieval world gave a theological justification to the feudal structure: it cannot be that nobility comes from Japheth, servitude from Ham, for in Noah's day no one was rich enough to keep servants, and in any case we all come from Adam and Eve. This carries the implication that "all men are born equal," though of course Enikel would not have understood it in a modern democratic sense. He is certainly not thinking here of the rights of the urban poor. But the patricians, the social élite of urban society, now felt strong enough to question the inherent supremacy of the courtly world. It is their voice we hear in the *Weltchronik*.

Enikel, then, was willing to shape his material, sometimes for the sake of his political agenda, sometimes just for fun. In itself, there is nothing unusual about this in medieval writing, but it is astounding to see what liberties he takes with Bible stories, where most poets of the period are particularly careful. Our extract from the Job story is an example of this. Like most narrative versions of the story, Enikel's is based on the first, second, and last chapters of the biblical book, but although he used the Vulgate, the Comestor, and very occasionally Honorius, the immediate source here does not seem to be any of these. He does claim to be following a source (13386), but such claims can be fictitious. Possibly he has the Latin Bible open on his desk as he writes, but doesn't consult too closely. At any rate, the dialogues soon develop their own dynamic, the two series of trials are completely rewritten to reflect what would be a calamity for a rich merchant, and elements of popular tradition creep in. The involvement of Michael (13216), for example, the guardian angel from Daniel 10.13, is also found in one Old French text, suggesting that Enikel has heard this somewhere, rather than that it is in his current source. The dung-heap is a normal element in medieval versions of the story, resulting from a mistranslation in the Septuagint (Greek Old Testament), but the stairway under which it is situated, which is so nicely illustrated in the fifteenth-century compilation manuscript cgm 250 (fig. 3), is Enikel's own idea, possibly borrowed from the Alexius legend, but in any case inspired by urban architecture.

Enikel's fondness for stories of corrupt Popes has been taken to indicate an anticlericalism, but this is unlikely as we know he had connections in the Church himself. More likely, we see here the tabloid writer's malicious delight at the discomfort of those in positions of power. For both of the Pope stories in our excerpt, Enikel's is the earliest account in the German language. Like many of his characters—even key characters—they are un-named, but we recognize them as Joan and Gerbert-Sylvester. Pope Joan is a medieval fiction, but Gerbert of Aurillac (ca. 940–1003), who took the name Sylvester II at his accession in 999, was a historical figure, a great classical scholar, credited also with introducing Arabic numerals to Europe. Rumors that he had his learning from the devil led to this cautionary tale.

Figure 3. The Devil tempts Job; Job under the stair. Compilation: Jans Enikel, *Weltchronik*, with excerpts of *Christherre-Chronik* (fol. 146v). Munich, Bayerische Staatsbibliothek: cgm 250, paper, 1410–30.

In most versions he is saved at the last moment, like Goethe's Faust, but Enikel leaves this open. The story of Saladin, which again Enikel is the first to tell in German, is likewise a popular tale which grew up around a real person, in this case the Sultan of Egypt and Syria (1137–93), who fought crusaders under Richard Lionheart. Despite his opposition to the crusades, Saladin had a very positive reputation in medieval Europe, and the story of his table is certainly not told against him. It belongs to a complex of related tales including most famously the parable of the three rings in Lessing's *Nathan der Weise*. It is interesting to study these stories from a motif-historical point of view, comparing them with earlier and later versions in other forms and watching a myth come to life.

The longest biography in Enikel's chronicle is that of Frederick II, the largest part of which is included in our selection. Since Enikel was born during the reign of this Emperor (lived 1194–1250), we are now moving into contemporary material. Our excerpt starts after Frederick's defeat of the Welf contender, Otto IV (1212), and his subsequent election (1215). Frederick is today regarded as a relatively enlightened ruler on account of his pursuit of liberal arts, his tolerance of Jewish and Muslim minorities, and his avoidance of a bloody crusade. However, his continued conflicts with the papacy led to malicious invective from papal propagandists, which is recorded for us by Enikel's Italian contemporary, Salimbene of Parma (writing ca. 1282). Enikel seems not to have been consciously critical of Frederick, and certainly he preferred the Hohenstaufen to their rivals, the Welfs, but nevertheless he takes over the most amusing stories from the opposition. This is why his words of praise in such verses as 28039 seem slightly inconsistent with the surrounding material. The stories told against Frederick include the medical experiment, which is also told by Salimbene—but Salimbene has only two prisoners—and the story of the assassins, which is related to Marco Polo's the "Old Man of the Mountain" and seems to be of Islamic origin. But the account also reflects the historical Frederick at many points, for example his love of falconry, a subject on which the Emperor actually wrote a book, *De arte venandi cum avibus* ("On the art of hunting with birds"). Frederick's excommunication belongs to the historically verifiable data. Frederick was excommunicated twice, 1227–30 and 1245, and Enikel records both instances, though he confuses some of the details. Frederick was King of Sicily before he became Emperor, and Pope Gregory IX, apparently alarmed at the increase in imperial power which would result from the integration of Sicily into the Empire, plotted to annex Sicily himself. Frederick was to be sent on a crusade and the ban of excommunication was used to force him to go. While he was in the east, papal armies were to take Sicily. However, Frederick managed to liberate

Figure 4. Silvester-Gerbert plays backgammon. Compilation: *Christherre-Chronik*, with excerpts of Jans Enikel, *Weltchronik* (fol. 195v). Munich, Bayerische Staats-bibliothek: cgm 5, vellum, ca. 1370.

Jerusalem by diplomacy, his crusade was bloodless, and he was back in Italy in time to defend Sicily. The Pope was forced to lift the ban. His second ex-communication, however, was never lifted.

The focus on the Duke of Austria, confusingly also a Frederick II, reflects Enikel's local patriotism. "Frederick the Warlike" more than once found himself in conflict with the emperor. In presenting the two name-sakes as initial antagonists who came to a position of mutual admiration, Enikel is representing Viennese interests. This story must have seemed important to him, as he repeats it almost word for word in the *Fürstenbuch*, which gives us a useful second take on verses where the *Weltchronik* manu-script appears corrupt (e.g., 28546). It is interesting that it contains one of the earliest references to the colors of the Austrian flag, red-white-red (28542 ff.), which seem to have been an innovation of Duke Frederick.

Emperor Frederick's death in 1250 marks the end of the chronicle. In chronicles which are completed, it is useful to notice how they end, as this reflects the historiographical understanding of the author. The "end of history" has been the focus of more than one major contribution to chronicle research. A religious writer might end with an abstract consideration of divine revelation in history, or with a look ahead to the end-times, or possibly with a hymn of praise. A secular writer might focus on the greatness of the ruler or city which his work is intended to extol. Enikel has ended his chronicle two decades before his date of writing, possibly because the intervening decades were not good ones for Vienna. Unlike Rudolf, Enikel is not writing with a program of Hohenstaufen legitimation; by 1272, the Hohenstaufen dynasty was a lost cause. But the Hapsburgs had not yet become established, and in these troubled years of political instability and apocalyptic preaching, many were nostalgic for the days of the last strong emperor, Frederick II. Rumors that he was still alive are recorded elsewhere, for example in a *continuatio* of the *Sächsische Weltchronik*, and are a typical reaction to the loss of a powerful ruler, for tales of kings who lie sleeping and will return are common (Arthur, Charlemagne, Barbarossa) and mirror the belief in the second coming of Christ; all are associated with the end of history. Without making any kind of theological statement, Enikel draws on a current of emotion typical of the years in which he is writing, and leaves us with this, his final word on emperors, on the world he knew, and indeed on all of human history.

CHRONOLOGICAL OVERVIEW

11th century	<ul><li>Lampert von Hersfeld, *Annales* (Latin), 1077–79.</li><li>Marianus Scotus, *Chronicon Universale* (Latin), died 1083.</li><li>*Annolied*, ca. 1087.</li><li>Frutolf von Michelsberg, *Chronicon universale* (Latin), died 1103.</li></ul>
12th century	<ul><li>Ekkehard von Aura, *Chronicon universale* (Latin), 1107.</li><li>Honorius Augustodunensis, *Imago mundi* (Latin), early 12th century.</li><li>*Kaiserchronik*, 1140s or 50s.</li><li>Otto von Freising, *Historia de duabus civitatibus* (Latin), 1143–46.</li><li>Peter Comestor, *Historia scholastica* (Latin), died 1187.</li><li>Gottfried of Viterbo, *Pantheon* (Latin), begun 1185.</li></ul>

13th century	[*Mittelhochdeutsche Blütezeit*, 1170–1230.]
	• *Gandersheimer Reimchronik*, 1216.
	• *Sächsische Weltchronik*, 1230s.
	• **Rudolf von Ems, *Weltchronik*, ca. 1250.**
	• **Christherre-Chronik, 1250s or 60s?**
	• **Jans Enikel, *Weltchronik*, ca. 1272**; *Fürstenbuch*, slightly later.
	• Rudolf MS, cgm 8345 (vellum), ca. 1270–80.
	• Salimbene de Adam (of Parma), *Cronica* (Latin), 1282.
	• Jacob van Maerland, *Spiegel historiael* (Middle Dutch), ca. 1285.
14th century	• Heinrich von München, *Weltchronik*, early 14th century.
	• Compilation MS, cgm 5 (vellum), ca. 1370.
15th century	• Compilation MS, cgm 250 (paper), 1410–30.

BIBLIOGRAPHY

1. TEXTS AND SOURCES

Comestor, Peter. *Historia scholastica*. In *Patrologia Latina*, ed. J.-P. Migne. Vol. 198. Paris: Migne, 1844–64.

Ehrismann, Gustav, ed. *Rudolfs von Ems Weltchronik aus der Wernigeroder Handschrift*. Deutsche Texte des Mittelalters 20. Berlin: Weidmann, 1915. Reprint. Dublin: Weidmann, 1967.

Flint, Valerie, ed. "Honorius Augustodunensis: Imago Mundi." *Archives d'histoire doctrinale et littéraire du Moyen Âge* 57 (1983), 7–153.

Gärtner, Kurt, Ralf Plate, et al. Edition of the *Christherre-Chronik* currently in preparation.

Plate, Ralf. *Christherre-Chronik: Linz, Bundesstaatliche Studienbibliothek Cod. 472*. Codices illuminati medii aevi 29. Munich: Helga Lengenfelder, 1994. [Microfiche reproduction of the manuscript with accompanying booklet.]

Rudolf von Ems: Weltchronik (Gesamthochschul-Bibliothek Kassel – Landesbibliothek un murhardsche Bibliothek der Stadt Kassel, 2 Ms. theol.4). Literarhistorische Einführung von Kurt Gärtner. Beschreibung der Handschrift von Hartmut Broszinski. Codices illuminati medii aevi 12. Munich: Helga Lengenfelder, 1989. [Microfiche reproduction of the manuscript with accompanying booklet.]

Strauch, Philipp, ed. *Jansen Enikels Werke*. Monumenta Gemaniae Historica, deutsche Chroniken III. Hanover/Leipzig: Hann, 1891–1900. Reprint. Munich: Monumenta Germaniae Historica, 1980.

2. GENERAL SURVEYS

Brincken, Anna-Dorothee von den. *Studien zur lateinischen Weltchronistik bis in das Zeitalter Ottos von Freising*. Düsseldorf: M. Triltsch, 1957.

Gärtner, Kurt. "Die Tradition der volkssprachigen Weltchronistik in der deutschen Literatur des Mittelalters." In *500 Jahre Schedelsche Weltchronik. Akten des interdisziplinären Symposions vom 23./24. April 1993 in Nürnberg*, ed. Stephan Füssel, 57–71. Pirckheimer-Jahrbuch 9. Nuremberg: Carl, 1994.

Günther, Jörn-Uwe. *Die illustrierten mittelhochdeutschen Weltchronikhandschriften in Versen: Katalog der Handschriften und Einordnung der Illustrationen in die Bildüberlieferung.* Munich: Tuduv, 1993.

Haeusler, Martin. *Das Ende der Geschichte in der mittelalterlichen Weltchronistik.* Cologne: Böhlau, 1980.

Hay, Denys. *Annalists and Historians: Western Historiography from the Eighth to the Eighteenth Centuries.* London: Methuen, 1977.

Knefelkamp, Ulrich, ed. *Weltbild und Realität: Einführung in die mittelalterliche Geschichtsschreibung.* Pfaffenweiler: Centaurus, 1992.

Schmale, Franz-Josef. *Funktion und Formen mittelalterlicher Geschichtsschreibung: Eine Einführung.* Darmstadt: Wissenschaftliche Buchgesellschaft, 1985.

Shaw, Frank. "Mittelhochdeutsche Weltchroniken—Geschichtsschreibung oder Literatur?" In *Chroniques nationales et chroniques universelles. Actes du Colloque d'Amiens 16–17 Janvier 1988,* ed. Danielle Buschinger, 143–53. Göppingen: Kümmerle, 1990.

Smalley, Beryl. *Historians in the Middle Ages.* London: Thames & Hudson, 1974.

Wenzel, Horst. *Höfische Geschichte: Literarische Tradition und Gegenwartsdeutung in den volkssprachigen Chroniken des hohen und späten Mittelalters.* Beiträge zur älteren deutschen Literaturgeschichte 5. Bern: Lang, 1980.

3. RUDOLF VON EMS

Brackert, Helmut. *Rudolf von Ems: Dichtung und Geschichte.* Heidelberg: C. Winter, 1968.

Ertzdorff, Xenia von. *Rudolf von Ems: Untersuchungen zum höfischen Roman im 13. Jahrhundert.* Munich: Fink, 1967.

Jaurant, Danielle. *Rudolfs 'Weltchronik' als offene Form: Überlieferungsstruktur und Wirkungsgeschichte.* Bibliotheca Germanica 34. Tübingen: Francke, 1995.

Simek, Rudolf. "Die Wundervölker in der Weltchronik des Rudolf von Ems und der Christherre-Chronik." *Österreichische Zeitschrift für Volkskunde* 43 (1989), 37–44.

Theil, Edmund. *Weltchronik, Rudolf von Ems—Karl der Große, der Stricker.* Bozen: Athesia, 1986.

Tippelskirch, Ingrid von. *Die 'Weltchronik' des Rudolf von Ems: Studien zur Geschichtsauffassung und politischen Intention.* Göppingen: Kümmerle, 1979.

Walliczek, Wolfgang. "Rudolf von Ems." In *Die deutsche Literatur des Mittelalters: Verfasserlexikon,* ed. Kurt Ruh, with Gundolf Keil, Werner Schröder, Burghart Wachinger, and Franz Josef Worstbrock, 8:322–44. Berlin: de Gruyter, 1991.

4. CHRISTHERRE-CHRONIK

Gärtner, Kurt. "Die Auslegung der Schöpfungsgeschichte in der 'Christherre-Chronik'." In *Die Vermittlung geistlicher Inhalte im deutschen Mittelalter,* ed. Timothy Jackson, Nigel Palmer, and Almut Suerbaum, 119–51. Tübingen: M. Niemeyer Verlag, 1996.

Ott, Norbert. "Christherre-Chronik." In *Die deutsche Literatur des Mittelalters: Verfasserlexikon*, ed. Kurt Ruh, with Gundolf Keil, Werner Schröder, Burghart Wachinger, and Franz Josef Worstbrock, 1:1213–17. Berlin: de Gruyter, 1978.

Plate, Ralf. *Die Überlieferung der 'Christherre-Chronik.'* Wissensliteratur im Mittelalter 28. Wiesbaden: L. Reichert, forthcoming.

Schwabbauer, Monika. *Profangeschichte in der Heilsgeschichte: Quellenuntersuchungen zu den Incidentien der 'Christherre-Chronik.'* Vestigia Bibliae 15/16. Bern: P. Lang, 1996.

5. ENIKEL

Dunphy, R. Graeme. *Daz was ein michel wunder: The Presentation of Old Testament Material in Jans Enikel's Weltchronik*. Göppingen: Kümmerle, 1998.

———. "Images of the Emperor Frederick II in the Universal Chronicle of Jansen Enikel." *Amsterdamer Beiträge zur älteren Germanistik* 40 (1994), 139–58.

———. "Der Ritter mit dem Hemd: Drei Fassungen einer mittelalterlichen Erzählung." *Germanisch-Romanische Monatsschrift* 49 (1999), 1–18.

Hellmuth, Leopold. *Die Assassinenlegende in der österreichischen Geschichtsdichtung des Mittelalters*. Vienna: Verlag der Österreichischen Akademie der Wissenschaften, 1988.

Liebertz-Grün, Ursula. *Das andere Mittelalter: Erzählte Geschichtserkenntnis um 1300. Studien zu Ottokar von Steiermark, Jans Enikel, Seifried Helbling*. Forschungen zur Geschichte der älteren deutschen Literatur 5. Munich: W. Fink, 1984.

Shaw, Frank. "The Good Old Days of the Babenberg Dukes." In *Bristol Austrian Studies*, ed. Brian Keith-Smith, 1–18. Bristol German Studies 2. Bristol: Univ. of Bristol Press, 1990.

6. THEMATIC APPROACHES

Abulafia, David. *Frederick II: A Medieval Emperor*. London: Allen Lane, 1988.

Besserman, Lawrence L. *The Legend of Job in the Middle Ages*. Cambridge: Harvard Univ. Press, 1979.

Boureau, Alain. *The Myth of Pope Joan*. Trans. Lydia G. Cochrane. Chicago: Univ. of Chicago Press, 2001.

Erffa, Hans Martin von. *Ikonologie der Genesis: Die christlichen Bildthemen aus dem Alten Testament und ihre Quellen*. Munich: Deutscher Kunstverlag, 1989–95.

Friedman, John Block. *The Monstrous Races in Medieval Art and Thought*. Cambridge, Mass.: Harvard Univ. Press, 1981.

Harvey, P. D. A. *Mappa Mundi: The Hereford World Map*. Toronto: Univ. of Toronto Press, 1996.

Murdoch, Brian. *Adam's Grace: Fall and Redemption in Medieval Literature*. Cambridge: D. S. Brewer, 2000.

Karl Schulteß. *Die Sagen über Silvester II (Gerbert)*. Sammlung gemeinverständlicher wissenschaftlicher Vorträge, Neue Folge, VII. Serie, Heft 167. Hamburg: Richter, 1893.

TEXTS AND TRANSLATIONS

WELTCHRONIK, Rudolf von Ems

(1–188)

R ichter Got, herre ubir alle kraft,
V ogt himilschir herschaft,
O b allin kreften swebit din kraft:
D es lobit dich ellú herschaft.
5   **O** rthaber allir wisheit
L ob und ere si dir geseit!
F rider, bevride mit wisheit
den der dir lob und ere seit,
Got herre, wan din einis wort
10   ist urhap, kraft, sloz unde ort
allir anegenge!
der anegenge lenge,
der ende trum din wisir rat
inder wisheit bestrichit hat,
15   dú noch mit anegenge nie
anevanc noch anegenge empfie
und iemir stete an endis frist
wernde in dinin kreftin ist,
mit dén din gotlichú maht
20   vinstir, lieht, tac unde naht
gescheidin hat und uf geleit
mit der momente ir undirscheit;
dú allin stundin alle zit
zil, undirscheit und maze git,
25   als ez dú witzebernde kraft
dinir gotlichin meistirschaft
alrest von nihte tihte,
geschûf und gar berihte.
    Dich lobt mit lobe din hantgetat,
30   die din gewalt geschafin hat:
erz engil und alle engil gar,
allir himile tugent, allir himil schar
mit lobe dienent dinir kraft
und nigent dinir herschaft,
35   dú sich hat an die hohsten stat
hohe uf kerubin gesat
und die tiefe der abgrúnde

WORLD CHRONICLE, Rudolf von Ems

[PROLOGUE]

        God our judge, Lord omnipotent,
        Regent, sovereign in Heaven,
        above all powers is your power.
        Every nation praises you for this.
5   Mine of all wisdom, may
        esteem and honor be yours!
        Prince of Peace, in your wisdom, grant peace and protection
        to the one who proclaims your laud and honor,
        Lord God, for one word from you
10   is the source, the power, the key and the origin
        of all new beginnings!
        The duration of all beginnings,
        the conclusion of all endings, your wise counsel
        has combined them with a wisdom
15   which even in the creation
        knew no beginning or commencement
        and always, without any end,
        remains firmly under your control.
        By this control your divine might
20   separated darkness, light, day and night
        and defined them
        moment by moment.
        These moments unfailingly endow each hour
        with its boundaries, its form, its measure,
25   as the discerning power
        of your divine skill
        conceived, created and commanded it
        in the beginning, *ex nihilo*.
           Your own handiwork renders praise to you,
30   the creatures you have fashioned:
        archangels and indeed all the angels,
        all the choirs of heaven, all the heavenly hosts,
        all bring their praises in your service
        and bow before your rule,
35   which has established itself in the highest place
        high above the cherubim,
        and has determined and measured

hat in kuntlichir kúnde
beslozin und gemezzen.
40 din kraft hat besezzen
ellú lebin darnah si lebint,
in lúftin und in wazzirn swebint,
uf erde lebent, vliegint, gant,
wurzint, wahsent, vliezint, stant:
45 dú nigent dime gebotte,
ir lebin lobit dich ze Gotte:
wan allir geschôffede geschaft
irfúllit hat din einis chraft,
si sin vol, ganz odir hol:
50 din sint himil und erde vol.
biz durh der abgrúnde grunt
ist wonendiz niht, ez si dir kunt
in sinis bildes figûre:
wan du Got der natûre
55 von anegenge gewesen bist,
als si getempirt hat din list
mit der vier elementen kraft,
die natûren alle geschaft
in der geschofede als ir lebin
60 in ir forme ir ist gegebin.
          Got herre, sit daz nu din chunst
bi dir ie was ane begunst
und anegenge nie gewan,
und doh wol mag und machin kan
65 anegenge und endis zil,
alse din gebot gebietin wil:
so wil ich bittin dich dastu
begiezest mine sinne nu
mit dem brunnin dinir wisheit,
70 der ursprinc allir witze treit;
und schoffe ein anegenge mir,
wan ih beginnen wil mit dir
ze sprechinne und ze tihtinne,
ze bescheidenne und ze berihtinne
75 wie du von erst mit dinir kraft
himil und erde und alle geschaft
von anegenge irdahtest,
in sibin tagin vollebrahtest
gar allir geschepfide undirscheit,

	the depths of the abyss
	with expert precision.
40	Your power has decreed
	what life each thing shall live
	gliding through air and waters,
	living on earth, flying, walking,
	rooted, growing, flowing, still:
45	they bow to your command,
	their life praises you as God.
	For every created thing
	is the fulfilment of your single life force,
	be they dense, solid or hollow:
50	Heaven and Earth are filled by you.
	Even beyond the floor of the abyss
	there dwells nothing which is unknown to you
	in its stature and form.
	For you have been the God of nature
55	from the very beginning,
	when your artistry blended it
	with the power of the four elements,
	shaping the natures of all beings
	at the creation of the world, when life
60	was poured into their physical forms.
	Lord God, since, then, your skill
	was always yours, without beginning,
	and had no commencement,
	yet is perfectly capable of giving
65	other things a beginning and an end
	when you speak the word of command,
	therefore I pray that you
	will now irrigate my understanding
	from the fountain of your wisdom,
70	which is the source of all knowledge;
	and create a beginning for me,
	for with your help I would wish to start
	to speak and to rhyme,
	to recount and to record
75	how in the beginning, by the power of your hand,
	you conceived in the first place
	of heaven and earth and all creation,
	completing in seven days
	all the divisions of created things,

80   und den stam al der menscheit,
        allin mannin, allin wibin,
        geschůffe mit zewein libin,
        und gebe nah menslichir vruht
        anevanc und urhab mit genuht,
85   und von der ersten stunde
        das dú menscheit begunde
        mit Adame dem erstin man
        wurzin und sich hebin an;
        und wie sin súntlich schulde
90   virworhte dine hulde
        durch sinis wibis tumbin rat;
        und wie dú selbe missetat
        an der nahkomindin art
        mit dinim slage irrochin wart,
95   do dú erstú welt zirgie,
        dú mit dén kindin ane vie
        dú von Adames samen
        anegenge und urhab namen;
        was sit dén ziln und sit der frist
100   geschehin und dén ziten ist
        das din kraft mit dem ersten man
        die welt hůp mit ir namin an;
        und wie dú welt ein ende nam
        und darnah dú andir kam
105   der stam, anevanc und houbit was
        Nôe, der lebinde genas
        inder arche, da im bi
        genasin sinir súne dri,
        von der geslehte und von der art
110   dú andir welt irhabin wart;
        und wie der welte name zirgie
        und abir dú drittú ane vie
        bi des heiligen Abrahames zit;
        und wie des kúnne wurtzete sit,
115   biz Moẏses, din werdir degin,
        began mit dinir lere pflegin
        des hers der israhelschin diet,
        do das her von Egipte schiet
        und du, herre, sůzer Got
120   in lertest dinir ê gebot
        uf dirre selben verte wege;

80	and created in two bodies
	the ancestors of all humanity,
	all men, all women,
	giving them by means of human procreation
	beginnings and origins in all abundance,
85	right from the first hour
	when humanity began
	in the person of Adam, the first man,
	to put down roots and grow;
	and how his sinful guilt
90	cost him your goodwill
	through the foolish advice of his wife;
	and how that same misdeed
	was visited on later generations
	by your chastisement[1]
95	when the first world passed away
	which had begun with the children
	who had their beginning and origin
	from the seed of Adam;
	what happened after those times and after that date
100	and during that period,
	how with the first man, your power
	gave the world its name and set it going;
	and how that world came to an end
	and after it the second arose,
105	whose progenitor, beginner and head
	was Noah, who survived
	in the arch, when with him
	his three sons survived,
	from whose progeny and from whose issue
110	the second world arose;
	and how this world passed away
	and again the third began
	in the days of the holy Abraham;
	and how his kin put down roots
115	until Moses, your great warrior,
	began under your instruction to maintain
	the army of the people of Israel,
	at the time when the army left Egypt
	and you, sweet Lord God,
120	taught them the commandments of your covenant
	on that same journey;

und wie si brahte in sinir pflege
Josue hin in das lant
das din geheiz in hate benant;
125 und wie si da beliben alwar
drizic und vier hundirt jar
bi dén rihtern untz uf die zit
das der edil kúnic David,
din kneht, din uz irwelter degin,
130 began des selbin kúnnis pflegin
mit kúnechlichir werdekeit,
bi dem, als úns dú warheit seit,
der drittin welte name zirgie
und abir dú vierdú ane vie
135 dú nah ir antreite sit
werte in ir ziln untz uf die zit
das si gevie der Babilon
durh ir gediendin súndin lon,
damit der vierdin welte zil
140 ein ênde nam mit wundirn vil,
und do mit namin den urhab
darnah der viunftin welte gab,
dú sidir werte unz uf die frist
dastu Got herre, sûzir Krist,
145 neme an dich die menscheit,
als úns dú Gotis warheit seit.
    Diz han ich minir willekúr
genomin ze einir ummûze fúr
und wil ez tihtin unde sagin,
150 und waz darzû waz nah dén tagin
das dú erstú welt virdarp
und do darnah Noe irstarp:
wie sinú kint wurdin zirsant
und wie si teilten dú lant,
155 wa si sih nidir liezin;
und wie die stifter hiezin
die in dén selbin stunden
dú lant stiftin begunden;
und wie dú lant wrdin genant
160 dar sih sit zinstin ellú lant;
und welhe kúnege schone
trôgin der lande krone
iê nah der undirscheit der zit;

and how Joshua kept the covenant,
bringing it into the land
that you had promised him;
125 and indeed how they remained there
for 430 years
under the judges,
until the noble King David,
your servant, your chosen warrior,
130 began to rule that same people
with royal dignity,
under whom, as the sources tell us,[2]
the third world passed away
and the fourth in turn began
135 which later, having been established,
continued in its appointed course
until they were taken captive by Babylon
as a right and proper punishment for their sins,
so that the fourth world
140 came to an end amidst marvelous events,
thus giving rise to
the fifth world,
which would continue until the time
when you, Lord God, sweet Christ,
145 took human form
as God's Bible tells us.
 I have chosen to undertake this
as a diversion,
and I want to rhyme it and tell it,
150 and also what happened after the days
when the first world passed away
and Noah died:
how his children were dispersed
and how they divided the lands
155 where they settled;
and what the names were of the founders
who at that time
began to establish countries;
and what the countries were called
160 which later received tribute from all the world;
and what fine kings
bore the crowns of those countries
even after the division of the ages;

                    wie in der drittin welte sit
165   Troẏe dú stat zirstôret wart;
                    wie von der hohin fúrstin art
                    die da warin sezhaft,
                    sit wrtzete ein andir herschaft,
                    die darnah Rome stiftin
170   und ir also hant giftin
                    das mit kúnechlichim werde
                    dú lant uf al der erde
                    dar dienstis wrdin undirtan:
                    des han ih mủt und gủtin wan,
175   ob mir Got der tage so vil
                    gan, das ih diz alliz wil
                    tihtin mit warheit, doh kúrzeklike:
                    welhe Rômesche riche
                    mit gewalte sit den jarin
180   biz an úns herren warin,
                    als úns mit rehte warheit
                    dú bủh der warheit hant geseit,
                    dú mit der heiligen schrift
                    sint des geloubin rehtú stift:
185   mit dien wil ih beginnin hie
                    der rehten mere, hôrent wie:
                    als úns dú schrift bescheidin hat,
                    da dú warheit geschribin stat.

(189–252)

                    In dem ersten anegenge—
190   ich meine nah der lenge
                    dú anegenge nie gewan
                    noh anevanges nie began—
                    geschủf Got himil und erde
                    beidú nah ir werde
195   mit sinir gotlichin kraft.
                    sin kraft geschủf alle geschaft
                    in sehs tagin, als ih iuh sage.
                    er geschủf an dem erstin tage
                    des tagis lieht und underschriet
200   lieht und vinstir unde schiet
                    lieht und vinstir, naht und tag.

       how in the third world
165   the city of Troy would be destroyed;
       how from the noble princely family
       which lived there:
       another ruling house would take root
       which would later found Rome
170   and bestow so many gifts on her
       that, by her royal dignity,
       the countries of the whole world
       would be subject to her.
       So I have the inclination and good intention,
175   if God grant me long enough life,
       to set all this in rhyme,
       truthfully, yet briefly:
       which Roman dynasties
       were in power from those times
180   until our own,
       as the books of truth
       have truly told us,
       books which, along with the Holy Scriptures,
       are the foundations of right belief.
185   With these I shall begin here
       the true account (hear it now)
       as we have been reliably informed by the scriptures,
       where the truth is to be found in writing.

[THE CREATION OF THE WORLD]

       At the very first beginning
190   (I mean after the eternity
       which had itself no beginning,
       nor was the beginning of anything)
       God created Heaven and Earth
       each with its own greatness,
195   by his divine power.
       His power created all creation
       in six days, so I tell you.
       On the first day he created
       the light of day and separated
200   light and darkness, and distinguished
       light and darkness, night and day.

do der ander tag gelag,
Got schůf das firmament zehant
das der himil ist genant,
205 nah sinir geschepfede undir scheit
dú himilschepfide treit
und davon lere und maze git.
an des driten tages zit
geschůf Got mer und erde und der fruht,
210 beidú nah ir art genuht.
der sternin louf, der umbejage
geschůf Got an dem vierdin tage.
vische und gefúgele und al dú dinc
dú meres und luftes umberinc
215 durh fliegende und durh fliezinde
sint und dú beidú niezinde,
geschůf Got und hiez werdin sie,
do der fúnfte tac gevie.
alse do der sehste tag irschein,
220 do wart dú gotheit inein
das sin gotlih gewalt
nah sinim antlútze gestalt
ein menschin mahte. das irgie.
das mensche lebindin geist empfie,
225 anevengic lebin und lebindin lip:
diz waz Adam, dem Got ein wip
mahte uz sinim rúppe sa,
dú was geheizen Eva.
dén mahte Got mit sinir kraft
230 uน̂dirtan alle geschaft:
tier und gefúgele und wilt und zam
machte in Got gehorsam
ir kraft, ir listin undirtan,
das si gewalt ir soltin han,
235 und swas uf erde krutis wirt
und an im bernden samin birt,
und ellú holz dú mit geน̂uht
in ir geslehte bringint fruht
ze nutzechlichir lipnar.
240 Got undirschiet die spise gar
und die fůre mit sinir craft

On the second day
God created the firmament
which is called Heaven,
205   which, in his creative plan
bears the heavenly bodies,
thus giving instruction and order.
On the third day
God created sea and land, and their fruit
210   in abundance, each according to its kind.
The course of the stars, their circuit,
God created on the fourth day.
Fish and fowl and all the things
which fly and swim through
215   the circles of the sea and of the air,
making good use of both of them,
these God created and commanded them to be
on the fifth day.
When the sixth day appeared,
220   the Godhead determined
that his divine power
should make a person
in his own image; and it came to pass.
The man received a living spirit,
225   the beginning of life and a living body:
this was Adam, for whom God soon
made a wife out of his rib;
she was called Eve.
God made all creation subject to them
230   by his great power:
animals and birds, wild and tame,
God made them all obedient to them,
subject to their power, their intelligence,
so that they should rule over them,
235   and all the plants which grew on the earth
which bore life-giving seed,
and every tree which bore fruit
in abundance according to its kind,
as healthy nourishment.
240   God divided the food for humans
and for animals by his power,

ze niezinne allir sinir geschaft
ie darnah als er wolte
das si die niezin solte,
245   und hiez si wahsen manecfalt
und gab ir wahsendin gewalt,
als in virhanchte sin gebot.
nah sinin werchin rûwete Got
darnah an dem sibindin tage:
250   nah gotlichir warheit sage
heiligiter den selbin tag,
in dem er rûwe und mûze pflag.

(253–401)

Dannoch do diz gar irgie,
Got hate noh geregent nie
255   uf die erde, und was och niht
menschin, als dú schrift úns giht,
das die erde erbeite,
wan das sih zerleite
ein brunne, der uz der erde ran,
260   uf die erde dar und dan,
so das dú erde nah ir art
gefúhtet von dem brunnen wart
und bernde schone in sûzir wis.
inder wolluste paradiz
265   Got das selbe mensche liez.
das paradiz Got werden hiez
aller erst von anegenge gar.
das paradiz mit frúhte bar
das schone holz des sûzú fruht
270   vil sûzú und senfú mit genuht
zezzenne und ze niezinne schein
und dem menschin niht entzswein
ze fûre und ze spise.
in des wunsches paradise
275   emittin an der miteln stat
wart das reine holz gesat
von des fruht wart irkant
swas gût und úbil was genant,
das ez das zeigite und tet irchant,

	to be used by all his creations
	according to how he wanted
	them to use it,
245	and he commanded it to grow abundantly
	and issued a decree
	authorizing its growth.
	After his work, God rested
	afterwards on the seventh day:
250	according to the Bible,
	he sanctified that same day
	by resting and taking his leisure.

[THE FALL][3]

	At this time, God
	had still never sent rain
255	on the earth, and also, there were
	no people, as the Scriptures tell us,
	to work the earth,
	but there was a spring
	which flowed from the earth, which forked
260	here and there upon the earth,
	so that the earth in its own way
	was watered by the spring,
	and bore fine, sweet fruit.
	In the Paradise of joy
265	God placed that same man.
	God had commanded Paradise to exist
	at the very beginning of creation.
	Paradise fruitfully bore
	the beautiful trees, whose sweet fruit,
270	seemed sweet and pleasant in abundance,
	to be eaten and enjoyed,
	and was not withheld from the people
	as food for their animals and themselves.
	In that perfect Paradise,
275	right in the very center,
	was the faultless tree,
	the fruit of which imparted knowledge
	of what was called good and evil,
	which it showed and made known.

280	swer ez az, das er bevant
	beidú úbil und gůt vil gar:
	das holz des obezzis fruht gebar.
	ein wazzir michil unde groz
	von der selbin mitil vloz,
285	das dem paradise gar
	luft und sůze fúhte bar.
	das teilte in vier teile sih,
	der vier teile ieglichir strich
	teilte sich dan in dú lant.
290	der vier teile einir was genant
	Phýson das wazir, das noh gat
	durh ellú lant in Eulat,
	des fluz das beste golt gebirt
	das iendir uf der erden wirt,
295	und das edil berdellium,
	das gůt ist, edil unde frum,
	das dú scrift úns nennit sus;
	der edil stein Onichilus
	da wahset ouh, in birt das lant.
300	das andir wazzir ist genant
	Geon, des fluz tůt sih irchant
	ubir Ethýopiam das lant.
	das drite heizit Thýgris,
	von dem tůt úns dú scrift gewis
305	das ez sin vliezin wande
	gein Asia dem lande.
	das vierde ist Eufrates.
	dú warheit úns bescheidit des
	das dú wazzir mit ir kraft
310	dé erdin machint berhaft.
	Got das mensche sazte do
	ins paradiz und hiez ez so
	das ez ein hůtere
	des paradisis were
315	und drinne hůte. do das geschach,
	Goi gebot im unde sprah:
	'swas das paradis gebirt,
	holz, obiz und das drinne wirt,
	das iz algemeine,
320	und mit das holz alleine
	das gůt und úbil ze wizzenne git:

280	Whoever ate it, knew
	both evil and good precisely:
	the tree bore the finest fruit.
	A great, broad river
	flowed out from this same central point,
285	which brought fresh air and water
	to the whole of paradise.
	It forked out into four parts;
	each of the four arms in its own direction
	dispersed into the lands.
290	One of the four parts was called
	the river Pishon, which still flows
	through all the lands in Havilah;
	the river produces the best gold
	to be found anywhere in the world,
295	and the precious bdellium,
	which is good, precious and useful;
	the Scripture names it thus.
	The gemstone onyx
	also grows there, the soil bears it.
300	The second water is named
	Gihon, the course of which can be seen
	across the land of Ethiopia.
	The third is called the Tigris;
	of it the Scripture relates
305	that it turns and flows
	towards the land of Asia.
	The fourth is the Euphrates.
	The Bible tells us this,
	that the might of these rivers
310	makes the earth fertile.
	God placed the man there
	in Paradise, and ordained
	that he should be a keeper
	of Paradise
315	and keep guard in it. When that happened
	God commanded him and said:
	"Everything which Paradise brings forth,
	wood, fruit and whatever is in it,
	you may eat it all;
320	except for that one tree
	which gives knowledge of good and evil:

in swelhir stunt, ze swelhir zit
du das holz izzist, du bist tot.'
alse Got das selbin holz virbot
325 fúr ungehorsamen mût,
er sprach: 'dem menschen ist niht gût
das ez gar alleine si:
machen im ein helfe bi,
dú im si gelich irchant!'
330 in disin stundin sa zehant
nam Got alle die geschaft
die er geschûf mit sinir craft,
und brahte si fúr Adamen dar
das er ir namin schûfe gar:
335 gefúgiln, tierin, wildin, zamin
gab Adam al gelich ir namin,
und als er tet ir namin irkant,
als ist ir name nouh genant.
      Dirre grozin ere,
340 mit der Got alse sere
das mensche hate geret
und mit wirde gemeret
sine werdekeit uber alle geschaft
mit sinir gotlichin craft,
345 nu hate der tievil zallir zit
haz mit zorne und grozin nit,
das dem menschin was irchorn
dú ere die er hate virlorn
durh sine valschin missetat.
350 nu began des tievils rat
daran gedenchin das das wip
vil lihtir gemûtin lip
ze gehin dingin hete
und das si baldir tete
355 nah sinem rate dan der man.
da bi gedahter ouh daran
das dem slangin was bereit
me liste und grozir kúndekeit
danne decheinim andirm tiere:
360 durh das frumt er vil schiere
den slangin zû dem wibe dar,
der do mit valschin listen gar
das wip mit kúndekeit betroug

in whatever hour, at whatever time
you eat of that tree, you are dead."
When God had forbidden that same tree
325   to his disobedient spirit,
he said: "It is not good for the man
to be so alone:
Let us make him a helper
who will be known as his equal!"
330   In that very hour,
God took all the creations
which his power had created,
and brought them before Adam
that he might think of names for them:
335   birds, animals, wild and tame,
Adam gave each in turn its name,
and whatever name he announced for them,
that is their name still today.
        By this great honor,
340   God so richly
honored the man,
and gloriously magnified
his pre-eminence over all created things
by his divine power.
345   Now the Devil was filled with an unending
rage, anger and fury,
that humanity should be chosen
for the honor which he had lost
through his wicked misdemeanor.
350   Now, the Devil's counsel began[4]
to consider that the woman
was of a far more casual
and flighty disposition,
and that she would far sooner do
355   what he suggested than would the man.
Furthermore, it also occurred to him
that the snake possessed
more craftiness and greater cunning
than any other animal.
360   For this reason he quickly sent
the snake to the woman,
there to deceive the woman
cunningly with crafty falseness,

und valscheliche das ane irloug,
365 daz si zirbrah Gotis gebot
und az das obiz, darumbe Got
beidú das wip und ouh den man
treip uz dem paradise dan.
Got únsir herre do besloz
370 das paradis mit hûte groz
dem menschin vor durh solhin zorn
das ez hate alse gar virkorn
sin gebot, das er gebot
an sine hulde und an den tot.
375 des wart dén schuldehaften drin
mit Gotis vlûche dannen hin
iemer durh al der welte lebin
ir gediender vlûh gegebin:
den manne, das er die lipnar
380 irrunge mit erbeiten gar
in dem sweize sinis libis;
des schuldehaften wibis
vlûh wart ouh vil swere,
das si ir kint gebere
385 mit erbeiten und mit grozer not;
Got dem slangen ouh gebot
das er slichke uf dén brusten sin.
durh disen wol gidientin pin,
das er die missetat geriet,
390 Got im ze spise uz beschiet
erde alle sine lebinde zit.
vientschaft, haz unde nit
sazt er sinem libe
zwischent im und dem wibe,
395 des er ir versin were
mit bizzen vil gevere,
und si des niht virtrûge
und sin houbit im zerslûge.
sus wart Adam und Eva
400 gesetzet uf die erde sa
und uz dem paradise getriben.

and falsely lie to her,
365 so that she broke God's command
and ate the fruit, for which reason God
drove both the woman and the man
out of Paradise.
God our Lord then barred
370 Paradise to humankind,
guarding it carefully, in such wrath
that they had completely disregarded
his command, which he had commanded
on pain of disgrace and death.
375 So the guilty three,
thenceforth under God's curse,
bore the curse they had deserved
throughout their lives in this world:
the man, that he would earn
380 their food by hard labor,
by the sweat of his body;
the guilty woman's
curse was also hard,
that she would bear her children
385 in labor and in great pain;
God also commanded the snake
that he should slither on his belly.
By this well-deserved suffering
(for he had instigated the misdeed)
390 God ordained as his food
earth, as long as he should live.
He filled his life with
enmity, hatred and envy
between him and the woman,
395 so that he would endanger
her heel with his bites,
and she would not tolerate this,
but would smash his head.
Thus Adam and Eve were
400 placed directly on the earth,
and driven out of Paradise.

(1491–1799)

Dú selbin kúnicriche
in Indya hant vierzic lant
und vier lant groz und wit irkant,
darinne manegir diete kint

1495

in aller hande geschepfede sint:
Garmanen und Orestas
vindet man da und Coatras
mit ganzen landen witen,
der welde in allen sitin

1500

die hohen lúfte rûrent
die dú himilzeichin fûrent.
    Dén selbin sint gesezin bi
die kleinen Pigmei,
in kleinim libe sere kranc:

1505

zweier getúmder eln lanc
ist das lút, das zallir zit
urlúge hat und manegin strit
gein chrenechen, die in leidis vil
tûnt. ubir drier jare zil

1510

gebirt das selbe lút sin kint:
alse dú sibin jar alt sint,
so sint si in ir altir komin
und ist in al ir kraft benomin.
bi dén das edil pfeffir wirt:

1515

alse das sin fruht ze der zit gebirt,
so hat ez wizir varwe schin.
vil wilder wúrme hûtent sin
biz das ez zitic wirt irchant:
so das geschiht, so koment zehant

1520

die lant lúte, als si sint gewon,
und tribent mit fúre davon
die slangin groz die man da siht,
und lant die beliben niht.
    Ein ander lút hat ouh das lant,

1525

die Macrobii sint genant,
groz an ir libe und niht ze kranch,
gewahsen zwelf klafter lanch,
die von dén krifin erbeit
hant, dén si ouh grozú leit

1530

tûnt mit manegin striten.

[WONDERS OF INDIA][5]

These same kingdoms [Gog and Magog]
in India have forty-four
large, expansive provinces
in which people of many races
1495   busy themselves with all manner of things.
The Garamantes and Orestae
are to be found there, and the Choatrae,
with their whole large countries,
on all sides of which the forests
1500   touch the sky
which bears the heavenly bodies.
These countries are the neighbors
of the little Pygmies,
small in stature and very frail:
1505   this race is just two cubits tall,[6]
and is constantly
at war and in conflict
with the cranes, which inflict great suffering
on them. At the age of three
1510   they give birth to their children;
when they are seven years old
they have reached old age
and all their strength is gone.
The expensive spice pepper grows in their land.
1515   At the time when it bears its fruit,
it is white in color.
The most ferocious dragons guard it
until it is seen to be in fruit:
when that happens, the people of the land
1520   come at once, as is their custom,
and drive away with fire
the great serpents which they find there,
and don't allow them to remain.[7]
That country also has another race in it,[8]
1525   called the Macrobii
large in stature and not at all weak,
twelve fathoms in height,
who have trouble with griffins,
on which they inflict great suffering
1530   in their constant conflict.

　　　　Indisin landin witen
　　nah ir lantmarche underbint
　　Agrocten und Bramane sint.
　　der geloube ist so getan:
1535　si geloubint ane wan,
　　so si in ir alter komin
　　und in ir jugint wirt benomin,
　　das in werde ein ander leben
　　mit einer ander jugende geben;
1540　unde brennent sich dur das
　　indem fúre, das in bas
　　nac ir alter núẃ jugend
　　kome mit uf gernder tugend;
　　und tȫdent sich durh solhe sitte,
1545　das si gejunget werden mitte
　　in widir núwir kraft irkant.
　　　　Dabi hant disiu selbú lant
　　ein lút das solhe site hat
　　das ir dekeinir das niht lat
1550　gůter noh ungůter,
　　si slahin vater und můter
　　so si beginnent alten,
　　ir krefte wider walten,
　　und gêstent sih ze wirtschefte mite.
1555　swelhir da virbirt den site,
　　der dunchit si vil gar unreht.
　　der sitte dunchet si so sleht
　　das si die fúr vermeinde hant
　　die vater und můter lebin lant
1560　biz das si selbin irsterbint
　　von alter und virderbent.
　　　　Vil lúte ouh indén landen ist
　　die ze spise zallir vrist
　　rou vleisch und rou vische hant
1565　und solhir spise sih begant
　　und trinchint das gesalzen mer.
　　das sih diz lút alsus gener,
　　das seit dú schrift der warheit,
　　dú von dén selbin landin seit
1570　das al da bisundir
　　sin egeslich merwundir,
　　halp menschen, halp tier irkant.

	In these vast lands
	near the boundary of their marches
	live the Agroctae and Brahmans.
	Their religion is like this:
1535	they firmly believe
	that when they reach old age
	and their youth has been taken from them
	they will be given another life
	with a second youth;
1540	and for this reason they burn themselves
	in the fire, in order that,
	after their old age, their new youth
	will be even better thanks to their eager courage;
	and they kill themselves through this custom,
1545	so that they will be made young, in which way
	new strength will again be known to them.
	Furthermore, these lands are home to[9]
	a race which has the custom
	that none of them, be they good or evil,
1550	will refrain from
	slaying their father and mother
	when they begin to grow old
	and lose their strength,
	and feasting on them at a banquet.
1555	Should any of them neglect the custom,
	they think him quite iniquitous.
	They so abhor this behavior
	that they regard as outcasts all
	who let their father and mother live
1560	until they die naturally
	of old age, and pass away.
	Also in those lands are many people[10]
	who invariably dine on
	raw meat and raw fish,
1565	and live on such food,
	and drink the salty sea.
	That they nourish themselves in this way
	is recorded in the trustworthy books,
	which also say of the same lands
1570	that every kind
	of terrible sea monster,
	half human, half beast, is to be found there.

Bi disin landen hat ein lant
ein lút, das ist vil wundirlich:
1575   dem sint die versennen fúrsich
gekeret: so si fúrsih gant,
die fůze hindir sich in stant,
da sint selzehen zeichen an:
beidú wip unde man,
1580   vater, můter und der kint
in solhir geschepfede sint
als ih nu han gesprochen hie.
    Da bi sint ander lúte, die
ze houpten hundis houbit hant.
1585   niht andirs si gekleidit gant
wand mit wildir tieren húten.
disen selbin lúten
ist menschen rede niht virlan:
man hóret si hundis stimme han.
1590   Ein andir lút ouh bi dén ist:
so des wip koment an die vrist
das si gebern suln ir kint,
dú kint an der gebúrte sint
in altlichir varwe gra.
1595   dú kint in alter werdint sa
swarz unde werdent gar
nah grawer varwe swarz gevar,
und werdent alt, noh elter vil
dan únsir alter habe zil.
1600   so si beginnent eltir sin,
sos îe gewinnent swerzern schin,
das nah ir jugent bischaft git
ir alters vollekomne zit,
als úns gebint dú grawen har.
1605   da bi ist ouh ein lút fúr war,
das ieglich wip ir kint gebirt
so si fúnf jar alt wirt,
und wirt das kint dan elter niht
wand so man ez gewahsen siht
1610   an aht jar, ez stirbit
von alter und virdirbit:
wand im niht fúrbas ist gegebin
altirs zit noh lebindis lebin,
wand als ich gesprochen han.

Among these countries is one inhabited[11]
by a race which is quite remarkable:
1575   their heels are turned forwards,
so that when they walk forwards,
their feet stick out behind them,
and are covered in strange markings.
Women and men alike,
1580   fathers, mothers and their children
have the characteristics
that I have described here.
Then there are other people who[12]
have dogs' heads on their shoulders.
1585   They clothe themselves in nothing other
than the skins of wild beasts.
Human speech is unknown
to these people;
they are heard to have the voices of dogs.
1590   Another race is also among them:
when the women reach the time
when they should bear their children,
the children are already grey at birth,
with the complexion of old age.
1595   Then, as the children grow older,
they turn dark-haired, and so take on
dark colors after the grey,
and grow old, far older
than the limits of our old age.
1600   When they begin to grow older,
they gain their dark appearance,
which, following the pattern of their youth,
gives them the full span of their old age,
just as our grey hair gives us ours.
1605   Furthermore there is in truth another race
in which each woman bears her child
when she is five years old,
and the child does not grow older
for when it reaches the age
1610   of eight, it dies
of old age, and perishes.
For beyond this they are not given
old age, nor long life,
except as I have recorded here.

1615	Mit warheit und an allen wan
	sint gesezen ouh da bi
	die wildin Arimaspi,
	die Einsternen, die Cýclopes,
	und bi dén Cenopodes:
1620	das ist ein wildis lút, das hat
	einin fůz daruf ez gat,
	der ist groz und alse breit:
	so sih an sinin rucge leit
	der man sor ungewiter siht,
1625	so mag ez im geschaden niht
	swenner den fůz ob im hat,
	der im vil clein iht schaden lat
	ungewitters komendin vluz
	und gerigens wazzirs guz
1630	und dabi sunnin hizze:
	mit alse vromder wizze
	das selbe lút im selbin git
	schirm und schattin zallir zit.
	dise selbe lúte sint
1635	snel und drete alsam der wint,
	swennez in iemir not geschiht.
	Bi dén ist, als dú warheit giht,
	gelegin abir ein andir lant:
	die da lantlúte sint genant,
1640	die sint ane houbit
	und houbetis beroubit,
	und in stant ane lougin
	an der ahseln vor dú ougin;
	fúr nase und munt hant si zwei loch
1645	for an der brust, darzů dannoch
	hant si vil wunderlichin schin:
	als ein tier und als ein swin
	sint si, seit dú schrift fúr war,
	ruch und geburst und vil gehar.
1650	Da Phýson vlúzit durh das lant,
	da ist ez Ganges genant.
	da bi ein lút noch wonende ist,
	das lept deckeiner genist
	ze spise noch ze lipnar:
1655	sin spise und al sin fůre gar
	an einis öpfils smacke lit:

1615	In truth, and without any doubt,[13]
	there also dwell in those parts
	the wild Arimaspians,
	the Monoculi, the Cyclopes,
	and with them the Cenopods.
1620	That is a wild race, which has
	one foot on which it walks,
	which is large and broad:
	when the man sees a storm,
	he lies on his back,
1625	and then it can do him no harm
	so long as his foot is above him,
	protecting him completely
	from the flood coming from the storm,
	from the flow of water from the rain,
1630	or indeed from the heat of the sun:
	with such a useful trick
	this race gives itself
	shelter and shade at all times.
	This same race
1635	is fast and swift as the wind
	when there is any kind of danger.
	In that region, as the sources say,[14]
	there lies yet another country:
	the inhabitants of this country
1640	have no head,
	no head whatsoever,
	and—no kidding—their eyes
	are positioned on the front of their shoulders.
	For nose and mouth they have two holes
1645	on the front of their chest, and also in other ways
	their appearance is amazing:
	they are like wild beasts, and like pigs,
	as the writings clearly affirm,
	shaggy and bristly, and very hairy.
1650	Where the Pishon flows through this country
	it is known as the Ganges.
	A race still lives in those parts[15]
	which lives on no kind of foodstuff
	for nourishment or nutrition;
1655	its only fare and its entire diet
	is the smell of an apple.

ze swelher stunt, in swelhir zit
ez smecket dran, ez ist genesen
und mûz von hungir sichir wesin,
1660   wand si damitte sih bewarnt.
so si von dem lande varnt
und ir mût stet iender hin,
den ôpfil fûrint si mit in
und smeckent dran fúr hungirs not.
1665   si siechint unde ligent tot
und sint verdorben sa zehant,
wirt in ein bôsir smach bekant:
das wirt ir lebins ende iesa.
      So groze wúrme sint ouh da
1670   das si, swa si die vindent,
ganze hirze slindent
und andir tier vil ane wer;
si durswimment da dú mer
mit grozir kraft her unde hin.
1675   Ez ist, als ih bewisit bin,
ein tier in dem lande alda,
das ist genant Zenocrota:
das ist vil kûne, vrevil, balt.
als ein esil ist ez gestalt.
1680   hals und houbit als ein hirz
ist, ob ir geloubint mirz.
lûwen brust und bein ez hat.
die fûze sin, daruf ez gat,
als rosses fûze sint getan.
1685   sin munt, als ih gelesin han,
biz an dú oren offin stat.
fúr alle zene ein bein ez hat
und ein groz horn, das alle wege
ist wesse und snidet als ein sege.
1690   menschen rede hat sin munt,
doch ist im menschen rede unkunt
also das ieman si virste.
      Ein tier, das heizet Cale,
ist in dem lande wonhaft:
1695   nah einim rosse ist sin geschaft
gestalt und in der groze wol
als ein ros gelichin sol.

	Whenever they smell it,
	at that very moment, they are revived,
	and are free of hunger,
1660	for they sustain themselves in this way.
	Whenever they travel out of the country
	or they want to go somewhere,
	they take the apple with them
	and smell it when they are hungry.
1665	If they smell anything unpleasant,
	they become sick and die,
	perishing forthwith:
	that is at once the end of their life.
	Such large serpents are also there
1670	that, if they can find them,
	they swallow stags whole,
	and other creatures, helpless before them;
	they swim through the seas there,
	to and fro, with great power.
1675	There is, so I am informed,
	a beast in that land
	which is called a zenocrota:[16]
	it is exceedingly courageous, bold and brave.
	It is shaped like a donkey.
1680	Its neck and head are like a stag,
	whether you believe me or not.
	It has a lion's breast and legs.
	It walks on feet shaped like
	the feet of a stallion.
1685	Its mouth, so I have read,
	opens as far back as its ears.
	In place of each tooth it has a bone,
	and a great horn which is always
	sharp and cuts like a saw.
1690	Its mouth is capable of human speech,
	yet it cannot speak a human language
	so that anyone can understand it.
	A beast called a yale[17]
	dwells in that land.
1695	It is shaped like a stallion,
	and also in size
	it resembles a stallion.

sin houbit und sinú wangin,
als sin munt hat bevangin,
1700 sint als einim bern irkant.
hinder als ein helfant
ist mit warheit sunder wan
gestalt sin zagil und getan.
ez hat ouh zwei vil wessú horn,
1705 dú sint geleichig: so der zorn
das tier begriffet, sa zehant
tût ez werlichen strit irchant
und reckit inwerlichir kúr
gein wer das eine horn hin fúr,
1710 das ander lit im hindir sih;
als ez slac oder der stich
gemachit mûde, ez bútet dar
das ander horn werliche gar:
sus tût ez mit dén hornnin sin
1715 zwivalte wer mit kreftin schin:
des kan sich nieman im gewern:
uf erde, in wazzern und inmern
mag ez beidú tag und naht
geliche wol mit wernder maht
1720 mit vorhtelichin sitin gar.
das tier ist groz und swarz gevar.
    Da sint ouh wildú rinder,
dú beidú vor und hindir
geburst sint widir hare.
1725 in zornlicher vare
ir mût gein allin tieren stat.
der rinder iegeliches hat
bi witem munde houbit groz.
gein wer uf grimminclichin stoz
1730 wehsilt ez ouh beidú horn,
swennes begriffet rehten zorn,
und tût vil grozin schadin mite.
vil vorhtechliche sint sine site,
wand ez vil seltin zorn virbirt.
1735 gefûgit ez sih so das ez wirt
gevangin jung in kalbiz namin,
so mag ez nieman doch gezamin
unde mûz och wilde

	Its head and its cheeks,
	which contain its mouth,
1700	look like those of a bear.
	Behind, its tail
	—in truth and without doubt—
	is shaped and formed like an elephant's.
	It also has two very sharp horns
1705	which it can move. When the beast
	is seized with fury, at once
	it displays its ferocity in battle
	and in a warlike manner stretches
	one horn out in front of it towards the battle;
1710	the other lies back behind it.
	When the horn becomes tired with fencing
	or jousting, it offers
	the second horn for battle.
	Thus it can present its horns
1715	powerfully in battle twice as often,
	for which reason no one can withstand it.
	On earth, in the waters and in the seas
	both by day and by night
	it is supreme, by its overwhelming strength,
1720	by its terrifying habits.
	The beast is large, its color black.
	There are also wild cattle
	which both in front and behind
	are brushed up the wrong way.
1725	They regard all other beasts
	with dangerous fury.
	Each of these cattle has
	a large head with a wide mouth.
	When attacked, in a ferocious charge,
1730	it also alternates its two horns,
	when it is seized by a real rage,
	and in this way it can do great damage.
	Its habits are terrifying,
	for it is seldom that it is not in a rage.
1735	Even if it happens to be caught
	young, while still a calf,
	it still cannot be tamed by anyone,
	and must remain wild,

sin und in wildim bilde,
1740   als ez von nature hat.
      In dén selbin landen gat
ein tier heizit Manticora
bi disin grozen wundirn da,
das an dem antlútze sin
1745   hat menschen antlútze schin.
sine zene sint drivalt.
als ein lêu ist ez gestalt
und hat an im vil scharpfin zagil
in wesser spizze als ein nagil,
1750   damitez ofte schadin tût.
sin varwe ist rot alsam ein blût.
sin stimme slangin wispil ist:
sin gedône ist alle vrist
inmislichir stimme hel.
1755   sinú ougin sint im gel.
ez loufit balder dan mit fluge
dechein vogil gevliegin muge.
menschen vleischis ez sich nert,
das ze spise im ist beschert:
1760   swa ez das bejagin mag,
das ist sin bestir bejag.
      In disin selbin landin gant
rindir dú drú horn hant,
und rosse fûzze sinewel:
1765   dú sint ouh starch, ummazen snel,
so si beginnent zúrnin.
      Da sint ouh einhúrnin:
den inder welte nieman
mit mannis kraft betwingin kan,
1770   so starch ist er und alse balt.
sin lip ist alse ein ros gestalt.
hirzis houbit hat er vor,
das treit er vientlich embor.
sine site sint unsûze.
1775   er treit helfandis fûze.
er ist gezagil als ein swin.
emmiten an der stirnin sin
hat er ein horn reht als ein glas,
vier fûze lanc, als ich ez las:

              wild also in appearance,

1740   as its nature dictates.

                  In those same lands there is

              a beast called a manticore,

              among all the other amazing things there,

              the face of which

1745   has the appearance of a human face.

              It has three rows of teeth.

              It has the form of a lion,

              and has a very sharp tail,

              pointed more sharply than a nail,

1750   with which it often does damage.

              In color it is as red as blood.

              Its voice is like a snake's hissing:

              its tone is at all times

              a variety of clear notes.

1755   Its eyes are pale.

              It runs faster than in flight

              any bird can fly.

              It feeds on human flesh,

              this is allotted to him as food:

1760   wherever it can prey on this,

              this is its favorite prey.

                  In these same lands there are

              cattle which have three horns

              and round feet like stallions.

1765   They are also strong, incredibly powerful,

              when they become enraged.

                  There are also unicorns:

              no one in the world

              can overpower one with human strength,

1770   so strong is it, and so fast.

              Its body is shaped like a stallion.

              It has the head of a stag,

              held high, aggressively.

              Its manner is hostile.

1775   It has the feet of an elephant

              and the tail of a pig.

              In the middle of its forehead

              it has a horn which is like glass,

              four feet long, so I have read:

1780   vor dem kan sih niht irwern
           noh mit dekeinir wer genern:
           alse úbil ist das selbe tier,
           so starch, so zûrnic und so fier
           ist ez und also unverzaget
1785   das ez niht wand ein reinú magit
           gevahin mag: swie das geschiht
           das ez die magt vor im irsicht
           sitzen, so wirt sin milte groz:
           ez leit sin houbit in ir schoz
1790   und rûwet bi ir schone,
           ir kúschekeit ze lone:
           sus vahet man in uf der lip.
           ist abir das si ist ein wip
           und megde namin ir selbin giht,
1795   so lat er si genesin niht
           und zeigit an ir grozin zorn:
           durh si so stichet er das horn
           und richet an ir die valscheit
           die si von ir selber seit.

1780 nothing can stand up against it
   nor defend itself in any way.
   So fearsome is this beast,
   so strong, so irascible, so majestic,
   and so courageous is it,
1785 that only a pure maiden
   can catch it: whenever
   it sees the maid sitting before it,
   it becomes quite gentle:
   it lays its head in her lap
1790 and rests in her care,
   as a reward for her chastity;
   and thus they use her to catch it.
   However, if she is no longer a virgin,
   and yet claims for herself the title "maiden,"
1795 it will not let her live,
   but shows her great fury:
   it bores her through with its horn,
   and visits on her the falsehood
   which she has spoken of herself.

CHRISTHERRE-CHRONIK

(7901–8010)

       Jacob nach sinis vatir bete
       leiste sin gebot und tete
       so daz er sumite nicht me.
       gein Aram in Bersabee
7905   vur er, als im geraten wart.
       durch Chananeam was sin vart,
       ein lant daz man sus nande.
       di lute von dem lande
       er vil vorchtlichen intsaz.
7910   si trugen sinem vatir haz.
       diz selbe vorchter an in.
       di stat zu Charjatjarim
       umbe vur er und kam sa
       einis abindes zu Luza.
7915   da wart er sinir rue in ein.
       er leite sin houbit uf einin stein,
       wan er grozer sorge phlac.
       doch wi unsamfte er lac
       in manigen sorgen tief,
7920   so virgaz er unde intslief.
         Nu daz er hatte sich geleit
       nach siner muede· und arbeit
       und in der slaf ubirwant,
       in troume sach der wigant
7925   in slafe ligende hi
       eine leitere von himele, di
       biz uf di erde reichte.
       di sine sorge weichte,
       und sach an der ubir al
7930   engele stigen uf und zu tal
       von im und abir zuzim wider
       di leitere uf und nider.
       als erz in sime troume *maz,*
7933a   *Zu oberst an der leitere saz*
7933b   *Got unser herre unde* sach
       von himele her nider und sprach:

THE 'CHRISTHERRE' CHRONICLE[1]

[THEOPHANY AT BETHEL]

In obedience to his father,
Jacob did as he had been told
and did not hesitate.
He went to Aram in Beersheba

7905 as he had been advised.
His journey took him through Canaan,
a country which bore this name.
He was very much afraid of
the people of this country.

7910 They had a grudge against his father.
This was why he was afraid of them.
He avoided the city of Kiriath-Jearim
and came instead
one evening to Luz.

7915 There he rested.
He laid his head on a stone,
for he was deeply troubled.
Yet, as uncomfortable as his bed was,
and despite his many worries,

7920 he forgot it all and fell asleep.
Now that he had lain down
after his wearisome journey,
and succumbed to sleep,
the warrior saw in a dream

7925 as he lay there asleep,
a ladder from heaven, which
reached down to the earth.
His troubles melted away
and he saw on its whole length

7930 angels ascending and descending,
away from him and back towards him,
up and down the ladder.
As it seemed to him, in his dream,

7933a at the top of the ladder sat
7933b God our Lord and looked
down from heaven and said:

7935 'ich bin iz, Abrahamis Got
und Ysaagis. ich wil in din gebot
gebin· und in din hant
zu besitzende diz lant
und nach dir dem kunne din.
7940 din geleite wil ich sin
und mit vride dich bewarn
uf dem wege, da du wilt varn,
und din mit selden pflegin.
Abrahamis und Ysaagis segin
7945 sol dir bereitit sin von mir
also daz gesegint an dir
suln in dinem samen werdin
di geslechte uf allin erdin,
und in dinem samen wil ich
7950 segenin· und bevriden dich.'
        Vvi der geheize uf der vart
und ouch sider vol vurt wart,
daz hat uns al mit warheit
di heilige schrift geseit.
7955 Got selbe der wolde pflegin sin
und tet im sine helfe schin,
so daz iz im zu seldin irginc
und zu wunsche, waz er anvinc.
ouch tet Got den geheiz irkant,
7960 do er vugete daz al daz lant
sinem geslechte immir sit,
in den tagen und in der zit,
do di Israhelische schar
Josue sider lange brachte dar
7965 und inz lant machite undirtan.
wi der segin solde irgan,
daz di kunne allir erden
gesegint solden werden
in sinem samen, daz irginc
7970 sint da di menscheit inphinc
Got unser herre Jhesus Crist,
der Got und war mensche ist,
in dem al der werlde kint
gesegint in sime gelouben sint
7975 der sin geslechte hatte irkorn
zu rechtir sippe, von dem er geborn

7935 "I am the God of Abraham
and of Isaac. I shall place this land
under your command, and place it
in your hand as your possession,
and your descendants after you.
7940 I shall be with you
and protect you
on the journey which you have to make,
and I will keep you in my care.
The blessings of Abraham and Isaac
7945 will be bestowed on you by me,
so that through your seed,
all the peoples of earth
will be blessed in you,
and through your seed
7950 I will bless you and keep you."
How the promise was fulfilled[2]
on the journey, and also later,
all this, the Holy Scripture has[3]
told us in truth.
7955 God himself protected him
and helped him
so that everything he attempted
worked out happily and to perfection.
God also fulfilled the promise
7960 when he decreed that all the land
should belong to his descendants for ever,
when the time came
when Joshua later brought
the people of Israel there
7965 and made the land subject to them.
How the blessing was fulfilled
that all the peoples of the earth
should be blessed
through his seed, that was fulfilled
7970 later when humankind received
God our Lord Jesus Christ,
who is God and truly human,
in whom all the children of the world
are blessed, through belief in him
7975 who chose his [Jacob's] line
as his own family, into which he was

nach der menscheite sint wart,
von des geslechtis reinir art.
   Jacob do er irwachte, her sprach,
7980   do er disen troum gesach:
'zware, Got ist an dirre stat.
des weste ich nicht. hi ist gesat
Gotis hus, und hi ist uf getan
des himels tor. sundir wan
7985   dise stat ist egelich.
daz ougit hi von Gote sich,
des genade mir geougit ist.'
uf richte er an der selbin vrist
Gote, der im da irschein,
7990   zu gehugede einen stein.
mit bezeichenunge groz
olei· san er dar uf goz
und wiete in. Gote geheiz er sa,
daz er im gebin wolde da
7995   den zehinden sinir habe gar,
unde immir wolde bringen dar
zu opphere sinen zehinden teil
und durch des hoen troumis heil
di stat mit opphere erin;
8000   swenner wider solde kerin,
daz er Gote eine stat alhi
buwite. daz ouch sint irgi.
mit grozir kostricheite
eine stat er da leite
8005   sint, di wart Betel genant.
die ist zu dute sus irkant
und mit namen "Gotis stat,"
wan si Gote wart gesat
zeinem urkunde der heilicheit,
8010   als di schrift uns hat geseit.

(8011–8230)

   Jacob von dannen kerte sa
hin gein Mesopotamia
und quam kurtzlich in Aram.
als er uf daz gevilde quam,

later born incarnate,
of his descendants' pure line.
　　When Jacob awoke, he said,
7980　　when he had seen this dream,
"Truly, God is in this place.
I didn't know it. This is the place
of God's house, and the gate of heaven
has been opened here. How truly awesome
7985　　this place is.
That has been revealed here by God,
whose grace has been revealed to me.
There and then, he set up
a stone to honor God,
7990　　who had appeared to him there.
With ostentatious ritual,
he poured oil upon it
and dedicated it. He promised God
that at this place he would give him
7995　　the tenth of all his goods,
and would always bring
his tithe there as a sacrifice
and honor the place with sacrifices
because of the great dream of salvation;
8000　　[he promised] that when he returned,[4]
he would build a city to God
on that spot. Later this did indeed happen.
At great expense
he founded a city there
8005　　later, which was called Bethel.
The meaning of this name is this:
it means 'City of God',
for it was built to God
as a testimony to his holiness,
8010　　as the Scripture tells us.

[JACOB'S WEDDING]

　　Jacob went on from there
towards Mesopotamia
and soon arrived in Aram.
When he arrived on the field

8015 da vant er sundir spil
      von schafen grozir herte vil.
      di hirten bat er do san,
      daz si im saiten ob Laban,
      sin oheime, lebite und were gesunt.
8020 si seiten im san zu stunt,
      iz stunde gar wol umbe in,
      und vurten in zu hant hin
      da er Labanis tochtere vant,
      eine mait, was Rachel genant,
8025 nach wunsche wol getan.
      zu der ginc er da san
      und seitir, daz si sin niftel were.
      si wart vro sundir swere
      unde kustin minnecliche.
8030 di vil edele tugende riche
      brachte di mere irm vatere do.
      der was sinir kumfte vro.
      mit vrouden er im gein ginc.
      vil vrolich er in intphinc
8035 und vurte in mit im heim.
      sin suzir wille im irschein.
      er vragite in manger mere,
      von welchin schulden er were
      alsus dar zuzim kumen.
8040 er sprach, do erz hatte virnumen:
      'du bist min vleisch und min blut.
      niman dir nicht leides tut;
      hi bi mir macht du wol genesin.
      durch mich wilt du vlizic wesin
8045 und phlegen der schafe min,
      di bevelich den truwen din.'
            Sus bleip er mit im da.
      kurtzlichen dar na,
      so ein mande hin quam
8050 unde der ein ende genam,
      Laban sinen neven vragite,
      daz in nicht betragite
      und ob er im dienin wolde,
      waz er im gebin solde.

8015	he found there—this is true—
	many great flocks of sheep.
	He asked the shepherds
	to tell him whether Laban,
	his uncle, were alive and well.
8020	They told him right away
	that he was prospering,
	and they took him straight
	to where he could find Laban's daughter,
	a virgin named Rachel,
8025	who was beautiful beyond words.
	He approached her
	and said to her that she was his cousin.
	She was quite delighted
	and kissed him sweetly.
8030	The most noble and virtuous girl
	took the news to her father.
	He was pleased about his arrival.
	Joyfully he went out to meet him,
	happily he received him
8035	and took him home with him.
	He treated him hospitably.
	He asked him many things,
	such as why he had
	come to him in this way.
8040	When he had heard everything, he said
	"You are my flesh and my blood.
	No one will harm you.
	Here in my house you will be safe.
	If you will work hard for me
8045	and tend my sheep,
	I will place them under your care."
	So he stayed there with him.
	Soon after that,
	when a month had come
8050	and gone,
	Laban asked his nephew
	(so that he would not grow discontented)
	since he was going to work for him,
	what he should pay him.

8055 Jacob sprach: 'ich dine dir,
wiltu Rachelen geben mir,
umbe si siben jare zil.'
'der dunkit mich nicht zu vil.'
diz lobetin si undir in al da.
8060 vil dienistliche dienter sa
Labane durch di mait.
di libe hatten dar virjait
mit vil ein mutigir minne
hertze, mut, sine sinne,
8065 und so gar, daz in dirre zil
nach ir nicht duchte vil.
sin herze was ir holt,
daz ir reinir minnen solt
im ringete gar di arbeit,
8070 di er in ir dieniste leit.
sinis hertzen senliche gir
so sere sich senite nach ir
unde e daz er ir impere,
daz im nach ringer were
8075 der dienst zwivalt durch sie.
von libe duchtin wie
dirre tage were nicht vil
des dienistis· und der jare zil.
        Do dise zit ein ende nam
8080 umbe sin dienist, sint er kam
dar, und im solde sin bereit
lon· nach sinir arbeit,
di er mit dieniste hette getan,
als ich e gesprochin han,
8085 nach der reinen meide libe,
daz si im wurde zu wibe,
Laban mit costlichir craft
machte ein groze wirtschaft.
sine besten vrunt virwar
8090 ladeter mit vlize dar,
da er ouch Jacoben wolde
lonen, als er solde,
sinis dienistis· mit der tochter sin.
do di nacht ir truben schin
8095 uf al daz ertriche brachte,

8055   Jacob said, "If you will give me Rachel,
        I will serve you
        seven years for her."
        "That does not seem too long to me."[5]
        They agreed this between themselves there and then.
8060   He served Laban diligently
        for the girl.
        His heart, his spirit, all his senses[6]
        had imbued his love
        with an enduring passion,
8065   so much so that he did not think
        this time too long to wait for her.
        His heart was so inflamed for her
        that the recompense of her pure love
        made the work which he did
8070   in her service seem light.
        The earnest desire of his heart
        yearned for her so painfully
        that he would sooner have[7]
        served this time twice over for her
8075   than give her up.
        In his love, it seemed to him
        that the days were not too many
        to serve, nor the years too numerous.
                When this time brought an end
8080   to the labor he had done since he first arrived
        there, and he was to receive
        the reward for his labor,
        after all the work he had done
        as I have already described
8085   for the love of the pure maiden,
        namely that she should become his wife,
        Laban hosted a magnificent feast
        at great expense.
        Indeed, he took care to invite
8090   his best friends to be there,
        where he planned to reward
        Jacob as he should
        for his work, by giving him his daughter.
        When the night cast its dull
8095   moonlight upon the whole earth,

als Jacob wante und dachte,
irginc nicht gar also.
Laban hatte eine tochter do,
di was Lia genant,
8100 "vluzouge", nicht schone irkant,
di was eldir under in zwein.
Laban wart kurtzlich in ein,
daz er im di brechte dar,
daz ers nicht wurde gewar.
8105 e daz er den morgen sach
und des tagis licht uf brach,
do sach er daz im was gelogen
und an der mait betrogen.
     Diz was im ungemach.
8110 do er Lyam bi im sach,
er trurte· und was unvro.
uf stunt er· und ginc do
zu Labane· umbe di geschicht.
er virweiz im, daz er im nicht
8115 sine tochtir gab zu wibe,
di schone, nach der libe
er im dinist hatte getan.
sin oheim antwurte im san,
er hetim gevarn mite
8120 da nach dem lantsite,
der were ubir daz lant also,
daz niman bi der zit do
sine jungere tochtir gebe hin
durch der eldern ungewin
8125 und e di geneme man.
Jacoben nach ruren began
daz herze und di sinne
nach Rachelin der schonen minne.
dar umbe lobeter im virwar
8130 noch zu dinen siben jar.
nach ir sin hertze bran.
durch si lobeter san
zu dienin· und nach ir libe.
Laban lobete si im zu wibe
8135 und zu gebene virwar,
swenner im gediente siben jar.

what Jacob thought and expected
did not come to pass.
Laban had a daughter there
who was called Leah,
8100 "runny-eyes," for she was not beautiful;
she was the older of the two.
On the spur of the moment, Laban decided
to bring her to him
without him knowing it.
8105 Before he saw the morning
and the light of day broke,
he saw that he had been deceived
and cheated of the maiden.
This distressed him greatly.
8110 When he saw Leah by him,
he lamented and was sad.
He got up and went
to Laban about the affair.
He reproached him that he had not
8115 given him his daughter in marriage,
the beautiful one, for whose love
he had served him.
Then his uncle answered him
that he had treated him
8120 according to the custom of that land,
which was practiced thus throughout the land,
that no one in those days
gave his younger daughter in marriage
to the disadvantage of the older,
8125 before she had taken a husband.
Jacob's heart and all his senses
yearned painfully
for the love of the beautiful Rachel.
So he promised him
8130 to work another seven years for her.
His heart was aflame for her.
For her sake, and for her love,
he promised to serve.
Laban also promised faithfully
8135 to give him her in marriage,
if he served him for seven years.

           Hir undir sprichit lichte ein man,
           der sichs nicht virsinnen kan:
           'was diz di irwelte diet
8140   Gotis, di er uz allin dietin schiet?
           und wurben di selbin do
           mit irn e wiben also,
           daz in daz wol inzam,
           daz er sinis ohemis tochter nam
8145   zwo? und was daz Gotis recht,
           und er doch hiz Gotis knecht?
           daz in kan ich nicht wol vristen,
           und daz wol mochte geschen.'
           ja! den wil ichs bescheiden:
8150   so vil was do der heiden
           lebende wider Gote
           ane e und in sinem gebote,
           daz Got sin vzirwelte diet,
           di er im selbin uz beschiet,
8155   wolde ouch sundir scheiden
           von den virworchten heiden
           mit ir e, mit ir wiben.
           er wolde und hiz si bliben
           in ir geslechte biz an di zit,
8160   daz er herre virkerte abir sit:
           bi Moyses, als man uns seit,
           und dar nach in der cristenheit,
           do der lute was worden so vil,
           daz si wol mochten ire zil
8165   zu wibe nemin unsippe wip
           und lazen der niftelin lip,
           al da virbot uns Got
           daz bi der zit was sin gebot,
           do der lute minner was,
8170   di er im zu dieniste uz las.
              Do daz zil an ein ende kam
           und sin dienst ende nam,
           Jacob wart sin lebin
           irvrouwit· und Rachel gegebin.
8175   di libt im, unde ir minne
           mit vrouden di sinne.
           si was im lieb und vil zart.

Perhaps someone who cannot
understand this will say:
"Was this the chosen people
8140 of God, which he chose from all the peoples?
And did they treat
their womenfolk in such a way,
that it seemed appropriate to them
that he took two of his uncle's
8145 daughters? And was that God's law,
and he was still called God's servant?
I certainly cannot defend them in this,
that such a thing could happen."
Yes, then I'll explain it to him:
8150 there were so many heathens there
living in conflict with God,
without the Law, and his commandment,
that God wanted to separate
his chosen people,
8155 whom he had selected,
from the evil heathen
with their beliefs, with their women.
He wanted and commanded them to remain
within their own kin until the time
8160 when he would later return as their Lord:
at the time of Moses, they say,
and later in Christendom,
when the people had become so many
that they were now well able
8165 to marry women not of their own families
and avoid union with their cousins,
then God forbade us
that which formerly had been his command
when the people he had chosen for his service
8170 had been fewer in number.
When the time had passed[8]
and his service came to an end,
Jacob's life was filled
with joy when he was given Rachel.
8175 He was fond of her, and her love[9]
delighted his senses.
She was kind to him, and very tender.

Lia hir undir swangir wart,
einen sun si gewan
8180 Jacobe dem reinen man,
der wart Ruben genant.
nach dem gebar si zu hant
abir einin, hiz Symeon.
der was ir hoen vrouden lon
8185 in irm herzen gein ir man.
den dritten gewan si san,
und der wart geheizen Levi.
ir herze wart sorgen vri
gein ir mannis vruntschaft,
8190 di gein ir nicht truk hoe craft.
des virden si do genas,
der wart geheizen Judas.
in rechtir zit doch schire
gewan si dise vire,
8195 di ich al hi han genant.
da mite si kindes irwant,
biz daz Got abir wolde,
daz si kint geberin solde.
Rachel alliz ane kindere bleip,
8200 daz an irm herzin virtreip
mit unvrouden hin di zit.
gein ir swestir truc si nit.
daz si so vil kinder truk,
als ich uch e von ir gewuk,
8205 diz mert ir ungemach.
zu Jacobe mit leide si sprach:
'dune wellis mir kindere gebin,
ich sterbe· und in mac nicht lebin.'
di rede duchtin ein spot.
8210 er sprach: 'ine bin nicht Got!'
'so tu doch daz durch mich:
durch kindere vrucht bite ich dich,
lege min diern zu dir
und gib mir vrucht von ir.'
8215 diz lobeter ir. si gab im sa
ir diern, was geheizin Bala.
di gebar im, als ich han
gelesin, einin sun Dan.

Meanwhile, Leah became pregnant,
and bore a son
8180   to that pure man Jacob,
a son who was called Reuben.
After this she soon gave birth
to another one, named Simeon.
He was her reward for the love
8185   she had in her heart towards her husband.
Then she had a third son,
and he was called Levi.
Her heart was free of care
about her husband's affection
8190   for her, which was not strong.
She was delivered of a fourth,
who was called Judah.
In a short space of time
she bore these four,
8195   whom I have named here.
After this she stopped having children
until God wanted
her to give birth again.
Rachel remained completely childless,
8200   and time weighed heavily
on her unhappy heart.
She envied her sister.
That she had borne so many children,
as I have informed you,
8205   this compounded her distress.
She complained to Jacob:
"If you will not give me children,
I will die, I can't go on living."
He thought these words were a joke.
8210   He said: "I am not God!"
"Then do this for me:
for the sake of our offspring I ask you,
lie with my maidservant
and make me fruitful through her."
8215   He promised her this. At once she gave him
her maidservant, whose name was Bilhah.
She bore him, as I have
read, a son, Dan.

nach dem gebar si abir im
8220   einin sun, hiz Neptalim.
hir undir gab im ouch Lia
ir diern, di hiz Zelpha.
di gebar einin sun, hiz Gad,
als noch von im geschriben stat,
8225   und abir do einin, hiz Aser.
Lia was in irm herzin her
und wante an den stunden
mit libe Jacob han virwunden,
daz ir diern truk di kint,
8230   alsi alhi genennit sint.

(8231–8258)

Bi der zit und diz geschach,
ein sintulut man kumen sach
in dem lande zu Achia,
di vil landes irtrenkte da
8235   und einim kunige, der was
mit namen geheizin Oggias,
der stifte Eleusim di stat.
di wart von im wol besat.
ouch saite man da me:
8240   sich lize ein mait bi eime se
vil dicke sehen, des sit gewis;
Lacus Irmonis.
sus was der se genant.
ir name wart sint irkant,
8245   man saite si hize Minerva.
di heizet di schrift anderswa
di kunstriche Pallas,
di urhab maniger liste was.
der kunst si von erste began,
8250   daz man wollin span,
—di wart bi den stunden
sus von den Criechin vunden
und mit den bleip si sit—
und larte do bi ir lebins zit
8255   so hoer kunste sinne,
daz si zu einir gotinne

After that, she bore him another
8220   son, named Naphtali.
Meanwhile, Leah also gave him
her maidservant, who was called Zilpah.
She bore a son named Gad,
as it stands in the Scripture still today,
8225   and another, named Asher.
Leah exulted in her heart,
and thought at that time
that she had won Jacob's affection
now that her maidservant had borne children
8230   as they are named here.

[10TH *INCIDENS*][10]

In those days when all this happened,
a great flood was seen to come
over the land of Achaea,
inundating large stretches of land
8235   during the reign of a King[11]
named Ogygos,
who had founded the city of Eleusis.
He located it advantageously.
Still more has been said of this:
8240   a virgin was often seen
by a lake, be sure of this;
Lake Triton,
thus was the lake called.
Her name was later known;
8245   they said she was called Minerva.[12]
Other writings call her
the skillful Pallas,
who invented many crafts.
She was the first to use the technique
8250   of spinning wool
—it was discovered by the Greeks
in those days
and has been known to them ever since—
and in her lifetime she acquired
8255   a knowledge of such high arts
that the Greeks, it is said,

Criechin hatten, als man seit,
ubir alle irdische richeit.

(8259–8302)

    Ruben Jacobis eldiste kint,
8260 als si hi benennit sint,
gienc einis tagis in einir snite.
er brachte nach liblichem site
eine wurtze, di ist genant
alrune. sinir mutir zuhant
8265 gab er di. do sis intphi,
Rachel was mit ir hi.
si hatte gelustliche gir
nach der wurcz. si batis ir
di swestir gebin. do sprach sa
8270 vil trureclichen Lia:
'hastu mir nicht gnuc getan,
dune wollis mine wurze han?
minen man hastu mir benumen
und lest in nirgen zu mir kumen.
8275 sol ich dar umme dich
lieb han?' Rachel sprach: 'nu wil ich,
daz er hinacht lige bi dir,
daz du di wurz gebis mir.'
daz geschach. si gab virwar
8280 Rachele di wurze dar,
daz ir wurde ir man.
si wart tragende· und gewan
einen sun, hiz Ysachar.
dar nach si abir gebar
8285 einen sun, Zabulon genant.
kindens si do irwant,
und gewan eine tochtir sa,
di wart geheizen Dina,
di si nach disen *sun*en truk.
8290 mer leides danne gnuk
mit clagendem smerzen
Rachel truk in irm herzen,
daz si unvruchtic bleip.

thought she was a goddess
over all the powers of earth.

[JACOB'S CHILDREN]

	Reuben, Jacob's eldest child
8260	as they are listed here,
	was out one day during the harvest.
	As a kind gesture he brought
	a root which is called
	mandrake, and gave it to[13]
8265	his mother. When she received it,
	Rachel was with her.
	She had a great desire
	for the root. She asked her sister
	to give it to her. Then Leah
8270	spoke full of sorrow:
	"Have you not done enough to me
	that you want to have my root?
	You have taken my husband from me
	and never let him come to me.
8275	Should I love you
	for this?" Rachel said: "I shall
	see to it that he sleeps with you tonight
	in return for you giving me the root."
	This was done. She did indeed give
8280	Rachel the root then,
	so that she could have her husband.
	She became pregnant and bore
	a son called Issachar.
	After that she bore
8285	another son called Zebulun.
	Then she stopped having children,
	though she did have a daughter
	who was called Dinah,
	whom she bore after these sons.
8290	In her heart, Rachel
	bore more than enough suffering,
	painfully lamenting
	that she remained unfruitful.

diz widermute ir virtreip
8295   Got, der ir clage irloste
mit sin selbis troste,
so daz si dem guten man
einen schonen sun gewan,
der wart geheizin Joseph. do
8300   wart si von herzin vro
und bat Got spate und vru
noch umbe einin dar zu.

This despair was taken from her
8295   by God, who eased her pain
with his own consolation,
so that she bore
the good man a fine son,
who was called Joseph. Then
8300   her heart was filled with joy,
and morning and night she prayed to God
for another one.

WELTCHRONIK, Jans Enikel

(13173–13456)

	Für wâr ich iu gesagen kan,
	ze den zîten was ein guot man,
13175	der was geheizen Job der guot,
	der hêt got in sînem muot
	ze allen zîten, swâ er was.
	der selb lebt und genas:
	aht und ahzic jâr wart im gezalt.
13180	dô er wart alsô alt,
	dô sprach got von himelrîch,
	man funde nindert sînen gelîch,
	der alsô guot wær alsam er.
	daz müet den tiufel hart sêr,
13185	daz er was sô reht guot
	und daz in got hêt in sîner huot
	und in sînem heiligen segen.
	der tiufel sprach: 'wolst dû mir geben
	gewalt über den selben man,
13190	wie schier ich in hiet brâht her dan
	nâch allen dem willen mîn
	und daz er liez die guottæt sîn!
	also wolt ich in betriegen,
	wan ich kan wol liegen.'
13195	zehant sprach got der reine:
	'nû hab dir gemeine
	den gewalt über den guoten Job,
	ob er zerbrechen well sîn lop
	und sîn guottæte,
13200	die er an im stæte
	hât gehabt sîn tag.
	zerbricht er daz, ez wirt sîn klag
	und sînes lîbes ungemach.'
	der tiufel dô wider got sprach:
13205	'er kan niht sîn sô stæt
	gegen dir mit sîner guottæt,
	ich bring in ûz dem lob sîn,
	sît ich sol sîn gewaltic sîn.'
	zehant er sich sîn underwant.

WORLD CHRONICLE, Jans Enikel[1]

[JOB]

	I can tell you a true story:
	in those days there was a good man,
13175	who was called Job the Good;
	at all times, wherever he was,
	he was thinking about God.

           I can tell you a true story:
           in those days there was a good man,
13175   who was called Job the Good;
           at all times, wherever he was,
           he was thinking about God.
           This same man lived and prospered:
           he lived for 88 years.[2]
13180   When he had reached this age,
           God proclaimed from heaven,
           that no one like him was to be found anywhere,
           who was as good as he.
           This troubled the Devil greatly,
13185   that he was so thoroughly good
           and that he stood under God's protection
           and had his sacred blessing.
           The Devil said: "If you were to give
           this man into my power,
13190   how quickly I would lead him astray,
           to do anything I wish him to,
           and to abandon his righteousness!
           In such a way I would deceive him,
           for I am rather good at lying."
13195   At once, God in his purity said:
           "Now I give the good man Job
           completely into your hands,
           to see whether he will abandon the piety
           and the righteousness,
13200   which he has shown with constancy
           all his days.
           If he does abandon it, he will be sorry
           and will suffer for it."
           Then the Devil said to God:
13205   "He cannot be so constant
           towards you in his righteousness,
           that I can't turn him from his piety,
           now that I am to have power over him."
           At once he took possession of him.

13210   do er schiet von dem heilant,
     dô sprach der heilant rîch:
     'ich erloub dir sicherlîch,
     vil bœser tiufel Sathan,
     über allez daz Job ie gewan
13215   ân alein über sîn sêl,
     der pfligt sant Michêl.
     sînen lîp solt dû niht tœten.
     welst dû in haben in nœten—
     daz urloup wil ich geben dir—,
13220   sô vinst dû an dem mann schier,
     ob er mir ist von herzen holt
     und ich im lieber dann golt.'
        Der vâlant dô verswant,
     des mannes er sich underwant:
13225   beidiu rinder unde swîn
     muosten dâ vor im tôt sîn;
     daz schuof zwâr her Sathan
     ze leid dem getriuwen man.
     der herter kom geloufen,
13230   der begund sich selber roufen.
     er sprach: 'lieber herr mîn,
     schâf, rinder und ouch swîn
     sint mir ze veld in grôzer nôt
     ûf der wisen all tôt!'
13235   dô Job des herters red vernam,
     er sprach: 'dîn leid und dîn scham
     solt dû lâzen varen.
     got gap uns bî unsern jâren
     sîn genâd hart schôn,
13240   des sag ich im grôzen lôn
     und lob sîner gotheit,
     mîn dienst sol im doch sîn bereit.
     als er dô wolt, alsô ist im geschehen,
     des muoz ich von der wârheit jehen.'
13245   Dô der herter von im gie,
     der tievel des dannoch niht enlie,
     er sant daz mort in sîn ros,
     daz si vielen in daz mos
     und den tôt dâ nâmen.
13250   er schuof daz in allen samen
     von im wê geschach.

13210	As he was taking his leave of the savior,
	the mighty savior said:
	"I give you complete power,
	you wicked Devil, Satan,
	over all that Job ever acquired
13215	except over his soul alone;
	it is in the care of St. Michael.
	You are not to take his life.
	If you wish to cause him distress
	(I give you permission for that)
13220	then you will soon discover whether this man,
	loves me with all his heart
	and whether I am more precious than gold to him."
	Then the fiend departed,
	and took possession of the man:
13225	both cattle and pigs
	lay dead before him;
	that in truth was the work of Lord Satan
	to hurt the faithful man.
	The herder came running,
13230	he tore his hair
	saying: "my dear lord,
	my sheep, cattle and pigs
	are in great distress in the field,
	they all lie dead on the meadow!"
13235	When Job heard the herder's words,
	he said: "Let go of
	your sorrow and your shame.
	Over the years God has bestowed
	his grace mightily on us.
13240	I thank him greatly for that
	and praise his Godhead;
	I will serve him despite this.
	What has happened is his will,
	that I know for certain."
13245	When the herder left him,
	the Devil still did not let up;
	he sent death upon his horses,
	so that they fell into a bog
	and died there.
13250	He made sure that every one of them
	was injured by him.

sîn kneht gie für in unde sprach:
'herr, dû hâst diu ros verlorn!
daz ist wærlîch gotes zorn.'
13255 alsô sprach Job der guot man:
'daz süll wir allez varn lân,
wan got der uns geben hât,
der gît uns an der selben stat
vich und ros, swenn er wil,
13260 wan er hât gewaltes vil.'
        Dô der leidic Sathan
sach an disem guotem man,
daz er niht wolt scheiden
von got: 'ich muoz dir leiden
13265 dîniu vil liebiu kint.
sît mich niht vich, ros und rint
frumt an disem guotem man,
sô müezen diu kint den tôt hân
und verliesen ouch den lîp;
13270 ich lâz niht leben dann sîn wîp.'
zehant daz ouch von im geschach.
Job gesach den ungemach:
dô sprach er: 'herr von himelrîch,
nu enweiz ich nindert dînen gelîch:
13275 dû gæb mir wîp unde kint,
vich, ros unde rint:
daz hâst dû in dînn gewalt genomen.
von dînen genâden wilich niht komen,
wan swer dîn genâd suochet
13280 und dîner gâb ruochet,
dem gît dîn gotheit, swenn si wil,
freud, êren und genâden vil.'
        Dô der leidic Sathan
gesach an disem guoten man,
13285 daz er an got wolt dingen
und nâch sînen hulden ringen,
dô muost der guot man hân verlorn
wîn, weizen unde korn.
dannoch wolt der guot man
13290 der gotheit niht ab gestân.
dô daz ersach der Sathan,
dô gie er zuo dem guoten man.

His [Job's] servant came to him and said:
"Lord, you have lost your horses!
this is truly the wrath of God."

13255 Job, the good man, said this:
"We should let go of all of this,
for God, who gave us it,
will give us in its place
cattle and horses when he chooses,

13260 for he is very powerful."
When the repulsive Satan
saw that this good man,
did not wish to abandon
God: "I must harm

13265 your beloved children.
Since the livestock, horses and cattle,
get me nowhere with this good man,
the children must die
and also lose their lives;

13270 I will leave none alive except his wife."
At once he did so.
Job saw the tragedy.
Then he said: "Lord of Heaven,
I know none to compare with you:

13275 you gave me wife and children,
livestock, horses and cattle:
now your mighty hand has taken it away.
I do not wish to lose your grace,
for whoever seeks your grace[3]

13280 and desires your gifts,
will receive from you, when you see fit,
joy, honor, and much grace."
When the repulsive Satan
saw that this good man,

13285 placed his hope in God
and wrestled to win his favor,
the good man next had to part with
wine, wheat and corn.
But even then the good man

13290 did not want to desert the Godhead.
When Satan saw that,
he went to the good man.

er sprach: 'wil dû dich an mich
lâzen, ich wil êren dich
13295   unde wil dir wider lân
allez, daz ich dir genomen hân.
ich wil dir sîn vil gereht:
vich, ros unde kneht
wil ich dir wider gewinnen;
13300   ich wil mit mînen sinnen
dir helfen schœner kindelîn,
wil dû mir undertænic sîn.'
dô sprach ez der guot man:
'allez daz ich gesehen hân,
13305   daz næm ich dar umb niht,
daz ich mit dir hiet pfliht.'
der tievel dô ûz zorn sprach:
'sô muost dû lîden ungemach
von mir mit grôzen nœten vil.'
13310   Job sprach: 'daz ist als got wil.'
     Zehant schuof dô der Sathan,
daz Job leides vil gewan.
er wart sô arm, daz ist wâr,
daz er sînen lîp gar
13315   niht gedecken moht mit sîner wât.
er gie an ein frömde stat.
er vant ein stiegen, diu was hôch;
einen mist er dar under zôch
und leit sich dar în an der zît.
13320   smerzen grôz, michel und wît
hêt er an sînem lîb genuoc:
vil blâtern er an im truoc;
ûz sînem lîb kruchen über al
maden vil âne zal.
13325   der hunger têt im grôz nôt,
daz im vil nâhen was der tôt.
er leitz vil dulticlîchen
und ruoft got an, den rîchen;
er sprach: 'reiner, süezer got,
13330   sît ich von dînem gebot
hân gehabt an ditz zil
guotes und genâden vil,
wâ von solt ich den willen dîn
zerbrechen, lieber herr mîn,

	He said: "If you will rely
	on me, I will honor you
13295	and will return to you
	everything I have taken from you.
	I will treat you fairly:
	I will get more livestock,
	horses and servants for you;
13300	by my arts, I will help you
	to have beautiful children,
	if you will be subject to me."
	At this, the good man said:
	"I would not take everything
13305	I have seen at the cost
	of having to deal with you."
	Furiously the Devil said:
	"Then I will cause you great distress;
	you will suffer terribly."
13310	Job said: "That is in God's hands."
	At once, Satan caused
	Job great suffering.
	In truth, he became so poor
	that he could not even cover
13315	his body with his cloak.
	He went to a distant town.
	He found a tall staircase;
	he gathered dung under it
	and lay in it without more ado.
13320	Great pain, intense and spreading,
	afflicted his body everywhere.
	His skin was covered with blisters,[4]
	and countless maggots
	crawled from his body.
13325	He was so tormented by hunger,
	that he almost died.
	He suffered it with the utmost patience
	and called upon God, the Almighty.
	He said: "Pure, sweet God,
13330	since by your command
	I have until now enjoyed
	good things, and much grace,
	why should I turn against
	your will, my good Lord,

13335 daz ich niht übel solt lîden?
ich wil dîn bot niht mîden.
dû wellest dich dann erbarmen
über mînen lîp vil armen,
sô lîd ichz vil gedulticlîch.
13340 herr, gip mir wan dîn himelrîch.'
        Dô der leidic Sathan
niht vant an dem guoten man
wan triu unde rehticheit,
dô wart im ân mâzen leit,
13345 daz er disem guotem man
mit lugen niht gesiget an.
sîn wîp daz allez ane sach
daz er sölhen ungemach
leit sô dulticlîchen
13350 durch got den vil rîchen.
si sprach: 'des bist dû wol wert.
dû wær ie der genâden gert
ze himel an die gotheit,
dâ von sô wirt mir nimmer leit
13355 swaz dir wirrt an dînem lîp.
mit jâmer dû vertrîp
beidiu naht unde tac.
für wâr ich daz sprechen mac:
daz dû dîn guottæte
13360 behieltest sô stæte,
daz muoz mich immer riuwen;
mîn kumber wil sich niuwen.'
der guot Job sprach zehant:
'wærlîch mir ist daz wol erkant,
13365 wil mir got helfent sîn,
daz ich überwint den schaden mîn:
von got mich nieman bringen mac
unz an den lesten tac.'
        Dô aber der leidic Sathan
13370 die red erhôrt von dem man,
er sprach zuo got dem rîchen:
'sich mac niht gelîchen,
herr, zuo disem guoten man;
er wil dir wesen undertân.

13335	to avoid suffering bad things?
	I will not thwart your command.
	Unless you choose to have mercy
	on my poor body,
	I will suffer it patiently.
13340	Lord, only give me the Kingdom of Heaven."
	When the repulsive Satan
	found nothing in this good man
	but faithfulness and justice,
	he was unspeakably angry
13345	that his lies could win no victory
	over this good man.
	His wife saw everything,
	how he suffered such
	distress so patiently
13350	for the sake of God Almighty.
	She said: "You deserve him.
	You always did yearn for grace
	with the Godhead in Heaven,
	and so I will never feel pity for you
13355	no matter what you suffer physically.
	You spend your time in lamentations
	both day and night.
	I can truly say
	that you have maintained
13360	your righteousness so constantly,
	that I must always regret it;
	my troubles are renewed."
	At once the good Job said:
	"This much I know for certain:
13365	if God will help me,
	I will overcome all that ails me:
	no one can turn me away from God
	until the last day."
	When the repulsive Satan
13370	again heard these words from the man,
	he said to Almighty God:
	"There is no one,
	Lord, to compare to this good man;
	he is determined to be subject to you.

13375   des muoz ich von im scheiden,
             ich kan im niht erleiden
             rehticheit und guottæt;
             er wil an dir belîben stæt.'
                 Dô daz allez geschach,
13380   dannoch leit er ungemach.
             hie merket, wie alt Job was,
             dô in der leid Sathanas
             sô grôz pîn leget an:
             von vier und ahzic jârn was er ein man.
13385   dar nâch macht in got künic zehant,
             als ich an disem buoch vant.
                 Dâ mit der vâlant von im schiet.
             got den guoten Job beriet,
             daz er gesunt wart und frisch
13390   sam in dem wazzer der visch
             und im die swer zergiengen
             und die blâtern die an im hiengen.
             dar nâch wart im an der stunt
             von got mêr genâden kunt:
13395   er gap im kint und ander guot,
             des wart er dô wolgemuot,
             und gap im ander genâden vil.
             freud, wunn unde spil
             gap er im an den kinden;
13400   sîn kumber muost verswinden.
             sîn armuot nam ein ende.
             dô ract er ûf sîn hende
             und danct der götlîchen êr.
             zehant gap im got selber mêr
13405   zwir sô manic schâf und swîn,
             fünfstunt mêr rinder unde wîn.
             er gap im guotes alsô vil,
             daz er hêt wunn unde spil
             an lîb, an guot reht als ein man
13410   der nie herzensêr gewan.
                 Dô daz Job ersach,
             er sprach: 'den grôzen ungemach
             hât mir got verkêret.
             nû merket, swer got êret,
13415   der gewinnet êren vil,
             ich mein, der im getrouwen wil;

13375	So I can only leave him,
	for I cannot sicken him
	of justice and righteousness;
	he is determined to remain constant to you."
	When all that had happened,
13380	he was still suffering distress.
	Now hear how old Job was,
	when the repulsive Satan
	so sorely afflicted him:
	he was a man of 84 years.
13385	After this, God soon made him King
	as I read in this book.
	With that, the fiend left him.
	God cured the good Job,
	so that he became healthy, and as fresh
13390	as a fish in water,
	and his pain melted away
	with the blisters on his skin.
	At once, God made
	even more grace known to him:
13395	he gave him children and other possessions,
	which he was delighted about,
	and many other gifts of grace.
	Through the children he gave him
	pleasure, joy and recreation;
13400	his troubles disappeared.
	His poverty came to an end.
	He raised his hands
	and gave thanks to the honor of God.
	At once, God gave him even more,
13405	twice as many sheep and pigs,
	five times as much cattle and wine.[5]
	He gave him so many possessions,
	that he had joy and pleasure
	from health and wealth, just like a man
13410	who had never suffered any loss.
	When Job saw this,
	he said: "God has averted
	my great distress.
	Behold, whoever honors God
13415	gains great honor,
	whoever, that is, will trust him.

daz ist an mir worden schîn:
schâf, rinder unde swîn,
ros, kint unde wîp
13420 hân ich von im und den lîp.'
dô er daz alles wider hêt,
als an dem buoch geschriben stêt,
dô ract er die hend gegen got;
er sprach: 'dîn heilic gebot
13425 und dîn heiliger gewalt,
der schînet an mir manicvalt.
dâ von sol alliu werlt leben
billîch nâch dînen hulden streben.'
      Sîn lop gên got wart manicvalt.
13430 er wart alsô mit freuden alt,
alsô daz sîn lîp nie
gegen got dhein unbild begie.
sîn munt, sin zung wart nie sô snel,
noch sîn ougen noch sîn kel
13435 gegen got nie sprach wan löblîch,
dâ von wart nie sîn gelîch.
sîn arm, sîn hend, sîn ruck, sîn bein
strebet allez hin gemein
gegen got ze aller stunden;
13440 die sæld hêt er funden.
dar nâch in kurzen zîten
wolt got niht lenger bîten,
er wolt sîn lop dâ mêren,
wan er im gap ze êren
13445 und ouch der werlt lôn:
er hiez in wîhen schôn
mit dem öl nâch küniges reht.
er was von reht gotes kneht,
wan er von gold ein krôn truoc,
13450 diu was edel und rîch genuoc.
dô hêt in got ergetzet wol,
wan er was ganzer freuden vol.
Job der lebt für wâr
hundert und vierzic jâr;
13455 dô nam in got in sîn huld
und vergap im sîn schuld.

I am a living example of this:
sheep, cattle and pigs,
horses, children and wife,
13420   and my very life I received from him."
When all this had been restored to him,
as it is written in the book,
he held up his hands towards God.
He said: "your sacred command
13425   and your holy might,
are manifoldly revealed in me.
Therefore, the whole world should live
justly, striving for your favor."
        His praise of God was manifold.
13430   Thus he grew old with joy,
so living that he never
caused God any offense.
His mouth, his tongue were never so rash,
nor his eyes, nor his throat,
13435   as to speak of God other than with praise;
in this, there was none to compare with him.
His arms, his hands, his back, his legs
all strove together
towards God, at all times.
13440   He had been richly blessed.
Soon after this,
God decided to wait no longer,
but to increase his praise,
for he honored him also
13445   with the recompense of the world.
He commanded that he be anointed
with oil, as is the custom with kings.
He was God's true servant,
for he bore a crown of Gold,
13450   which was precious and magnificent.
Now God had compensated him completely,
for he was full of joy.
Truly, Job lived
for 140 years;
13455   then God took him into his favor
and forgave him all his sins.

(22285–22678)

22285	Under den bæbsten gemein
	was einer unrein.
	ob die andern wæren
	reht mit ir gebæren
	und mit heiligem leben,
22290	ob in got die êr hêt gegeben,
	des kan ich reht gewizzen niht,
	wan got hât mit den rehten pfliht,
	daz weiz ich sicherlîchen wol;
	die rehten di sint freuden vol.
22295	Dâ ze Rôm was ein wîp,
	diu hête wolgestalten lîp
	und het sich gestellt als ein man.
	nieman für ein wîp sie kunde hân.
	diu wart ze bâbst dâ erwelt,
22300	wan man sie hêt für einen helt,
	der got rehter wære,
	doch was si wandelbære,
	daz si was wîp und wolt sîn man—,
	dâ von man si zi bâbst nam.
22305	waz si wunders dâ getreip,
	di wîl si bâbst dâ beleip,
	des kan ich niht gar gesagen,
	dâ von sô muoz ich stille dagen,
	wan einez weiz ich von ir wol,
22310	daz ich iu für wâr sagen sol:
	dô man der wîpheit inne wart,
	dô wart niht lenger gespart,
	man tæt sie fuder zehant,
	daz ist mir von ir wol bekant,
22315	wan si den spot dar umb enpfie,
	der ir an ir êre gie,
	und muost von Rôm scheiden.
	den liuten begund si leiden
	umb ir bœse missetât,
22320	die ir lîp begangen hât.
	Ze Rôm wart bâbst ouch ein man,
	als ich von im vernomen hân;
	wie ez dar zuo kæme,
	daz man in ze bâbst næme,

[CORRUPT POPES]

22285	Among all the many Popes
	there was one who was corrupt.
	Whether the others were
	correct in their behavior
	and lived holy lives,
22290	whether God gave them this honor,[6]
	that I cannot know for certain;
	but that God looks after the just,
	that I know for a fact;
	the just are full of joy.
22295	In Rome there was a woman,[7]
	who had a beautiful figure,
	and who passed herself off as a man.
	No one could have recognized her as a woman.
	She was elected there as Pope,
22300	for they thought she was a hero,
	who was righteous in God's eyes,
	but in fact she was fickle,
	in that she was a woman and wanted to be a man;
	and so they made her Pope.
22305	I cannot say
	what strange things she did,
	while she was Pope,
	so I must remain silent on that,
	but one thing I do know about her,
22310	and that I will tell you for a fact:
	when they discovered that she was a woman,
	no time was wasted,
	she was banished at once,
	that much I do know about her,
22315	for she was subjected to a ridicule
	which cost her her honor,
	and she had to leave Rome.
	The people grew to hate her
	because of the wicked misdeed
22320	which she had committed.
	A man also became Pope in Rome,[8]
	so I have heard,
	and how it came about
	that he was made Pope,

22325　daz hât man mir kunt getân,
　　　　dâ von wil ich iuchz wizzen lân.
　　　　er was des êrsten ein spilær,
　　　　aller tugend was er lær,
　　　　wan daz er wol gelêrt was,
22330　daz er wol schreip unde las
　　　　swaz man im vor zalt;
　　　　die niuwen ê und die alt
　　　　kund er gar ân mâzen vil.
　　　　dâ von ich niht verswîgen wil,
22335　ich well den liuten tuon bekant,
　　　　wie er bâbst wurd genant.
　　　　er was ein arm vlætic man,
　　　　wan der würfel gewan im an,
　　　　daz er was guotes alsô bar,
22340　daz ich ez niht gesagen tar.
　　　　　　Ze einen zîten er gedâht
　　　　daz in zuo der bâbstheit brâht.
　　　　er gedâht in sînem sin:
　　　　wie lang sol ich arm sîn?
22345　ich wil dem tiufel geben
　　　　sêl, lîp und mîn leben.
　　　　dâ mit er an ein gewick gie.
　　　　er sprach: 'war umb oder wie
　　　　sol ich armer hie bestân?
22350　ich wil dem tiufel mîn sêl lân.'
　　　　vor angst was im heiz.
　　　　er umbreiz sich in einem kreiz
　　　　unde ruoft dem tiufel dar.
　　　　dar kom er offenbar
22355　mit engstlîcher vart,
　　　　sô bitters nie gesehen wart.
　　　　er sprach: 'waz wil dû, loterpfaff?
　　　　dû bist ein rehter aff,
　　　　daz dû mich müest sô sêr.'
22360　der nakent man sprach: 'ich wil dîn lêr
　　　　gern haben umbe guot.
　　　　mîn armuot mir unsanfte tuot.'
　　　　der tiufel: 'wil dû mir
　　　　volgen, sô lêr ich dich schier,
22365　daz dû wirst ein gewaltic man

22325	that I have been told,
	and so I will tell you it too.
	To begin with, he was a gambler,
	devoid of any virtue,
	except that he was well-educated,
22330	and could read and write
	whatever he was told.
	He had a profound knowledge of
	the New Testament and the Old.
	I will not omit this,
22335	I want to tell the people,
	how he was appointed Pope.
	He was thoroughly poor,[9]
	for the dice gained such control of him,
	that he became so bereft of property
22340	that I hardly dare tell of it.
	One day he had the idea
	which would bring him to the papacy.
	He thought to himself:
	"How long shall I be poor?
22345	I will give the Devil
	my soul, my body and my life."
	So he went to a crossroads.[10]
	He said: "Why
	should I remain here in poverty?
22350	I will sell my soul to the Devil."
	He was burning with fear.
	He drew a circle around him
	and called upon the Devil.
	He appeared there visibly
22355	with a terrifying motion,
	as fearsome as has ever been seen.
	He said: "What do you want, you good-for-nothing priest?
	You are a complete fool,
	to cause me so much trouble."
22360	The naked man said: "I want you to show me[11]
	how to become rich.
	I have had enough of being poor."
	The Devil: "If you will
	obey me, I will soon teach you,
22365	so that you become a powerful man

und die kristen dir all undertân
werdent gemeine.
gip mir dîn sêl aleine,
sô wil ich dich mit sachen
22370   ze Rôm bâbst machen.
gip mir von dîner sêl ein lêhen:
wann ich dich süll an sehen
ze Jerusalêm in bâbstes wât,
und daz dîn muot ze singen gât
22375   ze Jerusalêm ûf dem altær,
daz ich dich danne mit swær
füer swâ ich hin welle,
in die wîz odr in die helle.'
    Do gedâht im der loterpfaff:
22380   tæt ich des niht, ich wær ein aff.
wan kum ich ze Jerusalêm,
daz mich dan der tiufel hin næm?
daz geschiht an mir nimmer.
ich bin frî vor dir immer.
22385   wer siht mich enhalb meres gân?
also gedâht im der tumb man.
dô west er niht die geschiht,
daz er daz Jerusalêm niht
meint, daz enhalb meres lac.
22390   daz was dem tumben mac ein slac.
er meint ein kleinez kirchlîn,
daz muoz stæt ze Rôm sîn,
und muost ein ieglîch bâbest zwâr
einest besingen in dem jâr.
22395   des enwest nicht der man.
er sprach: 'mac ich die êre hân,
daz ich werd bâbst und mug gesîn,
sô hab dir lîp und sêl mîn.'
der tiufel sprach: 'des gip mir
22400   dînen brief vil schier,
alsô daz ich mit dînem bluot
schrîb an einen brief guot,
daz der mîn wortzeichen sî,
daz dû sîst mîn und niht frî.'
22405   Zehant dem schuolære
was diu red niht swære.

and all Christians will be subject to you
without exception.
Just give me your soul,
and I will use my arts
22370   to make you Pope in Rome.
Make me the overlord of your soul:
when I see you
in Jerusalem, in papal robes,
setting your mind to singing the mass
22375   at the altar in Jerusalem,
let me then take you
in torment wherever I will,
to purgatory or to hell."
      The good-for-nothing priest thought to himself:
22380   "I would be a fool if I didn't do this.
When will I ever go to Jerusalem,
that the Devil could carry me off?
That will never happen to me.
I am free of you forever.
22385   Who will see me crossing the sea?"
Thus the foolish man thought to himself.
What he didn't know was
that the Devil didn't mean
the Jerusalem across the sea.
22390   That would come as a blow to the foolish man.
He meant a little church,[12]
which by all accounts is close to Rome,
and in truth, every Pope must
sing the mass there once a year.
22395   The man did not know this.
He said: "If I can have the honor,
of becoming and reigning as Pope,
you may take me, body and soul."
The Devil said: "Give me that
22400   in writing, right away,
so that I can write a contract
in your blood,
which is my guarantee,
that you are mine, and not a freeman."
22405   At once the scholar
was in agreement.

er stach in den vinger guot,
alsô daz im daz rôt bluot
dâ zuo dem vinger her ûz ran.
22410   dâ schreip der vâlandes man
einen brief mit dem bluot.
daz was dem schuolær niht guot.
er sprach: 'ich wil dich lêrn,
dû solt zuo dem bischof kêrn,
22415   dâ wil ich dich berâten wol,
daz dû wirst ganzer freuden vol.'
      Zehant er zuo dem bischof gie.
nieman in dâ schôn enpfie.
dâ stuont er ûzen an der tür.
22420   nieman liez in hin für.
des bischofs schrîber von im schiet,
als im der tiufel riet,
daz er gieng zuo einem wîn,
und trunk, daz er niht trunkner möht sîn.
22425   dô wolt der bischof an der stat
sînen brief senden drât.
er sprach: 'ir sült mir bringen drât
mînen schrîber in ein kemnât,
und îlet des baldiclîch.
22430   ich muoz in haben wærlîch.'
daz west der tiufel an der stat,
der in zuo dem wîn geschündet hât;
der liez niht vinden den schrîbær.
dem herren macht er in unmær.
22435   vil vast er ûz der kamer rief:
'wær ieman der mir einen brief
kund schrîben ze einer stunde,
sîn armuot im verswunde.'
daz hôrt der arm nackent man.
22440   'getörst ir iuch an mich lân,'
sprach er, 'ich schrîb iu sicherlîch.
ich bin gar künst rîch.
daz sehet ir wol an mîner hant,
und solt ez sîn umb ein lant,
22445   ir wært mit mir versûmet niht;
an mîner geschrift man daz siht.'
      Der bischof geloubt im gar.
die materje gap er im dar.

He pricked himself on the finger,
so that the red blood
ran out of the finger.
22410 Then the fiend's vassal
wrote a contract with the blood.
That was not good for the scholar.
He said: "I will instruct you.
Go to the Bishop.
22415 There I will advise you well,
so that your joy is complete."
    At once he went to the Bishop.
No one received him there properly.
He waited outside at the door.
22420 No one let him in.
The Bishop's clerk had disappeared;
at the Devil's instigation,
he had gone off for some wine,
and drunk until he couldn't have been more drunk.
22425 Just then the Bishop
wanted to send an urgent letter.
He said: "Quickly, bring
my scribe to me in the chamber,
and be fast about it.
22430 I have great need of him."
The Devil, who had driven him
to the wine, knew this at once;
he made sure the clerk was not found.
He made the lord furious with him.
22435 He bellowed out of the room:
"If there is anyone who can write me
a letter right now,
he will be poor no longer."
The poor, naked man heard this.
22440 "If you will take the risk of relying on me,"
he said, "I will certainly write for you.
I am very talented.
You will see that from my handwriting,
and even if a whole country is at stake,
22445 with my help you will not lose it;
this can be seen from my writing."
    The Bishop took him at his word.
He gave him the writing materials.

dâ mit schreip der nackent man
22450   einen brief, daz nieman
sô guotes briefes hêt gesehen;
des muost im der bischof jehen.
dô er den brief dâ gelas,
des getihtes er vil frô was,
22455   daz er was sô künst rich.
er sprach: 'ich sag dir wærlîch,
woldest dû daz würfelspil lân,
ich wolt mich umb dich nemen an.'
des swuor er im manigen eit.
22460   er sprach: 'ich wil mîn stætikeit,
herr, niht zerbrechen.'
do begund der bischof sprechen
zuo sînem kameræere:
'ring im sîn swære
22465   und gip im an niuwe kleit,
ob er mir biet sînen eit,
daz er well daz würfelspil
lân, wan er kan sîn vil.'
dâ für bôt er mangen eit,
22470   daz er wolt sîn stætikeit
dar an lâzen für gân.
dô gap man im kleider an,
von Îper daz beste,
daz ieman dâ weste.
22475   geriten macht er in iesâ,
daz ie man moht sprechen dâ,
er wær der baz geritenst man,
im wær bereit der êren van.
dâ mit er dient zwâr
22480   dem bischof wol ein jâr,
wan swann er begreif daz spil,
der tiufel in niht liez vil
verliesen, wan er in lêrte,
den würfel er im kêrte
22485   zuo dem besten nâch gewinn,
daz des nieman wart inn.
dâ von der schuolære
gewan âne swære
allez daz er wolde,
22490   wan im der tiufel helfen wolde.

	With these, the naked man wrote
22450	a letter, such a good letter
	as no one had ever seen before;
	the Bishop had to confirm this.
	When he read the letter,
	he was delighted with its rhetoric,
22455	and that it was so artfully composed.
	He said: "I tell you the truth,
	if you would only stop gambling,
	I would take care of you."
	He swore this oath many times.
22460	He said: "Lord, I will not
	be found wanting in my constancy."
	Then the Bishop spoke
	to his chamberlain:
	"Attend to his needs
22465	and put fresh clothes on him,
	if he will swear to me
	that he will stop gambling,
	for he is an expert at that."
	He swore many oaths on this,
22470	that in this respect he would let
	his constancy come to the fore.
	Then they put clothes on him,
	from Ypres, the best[13]
	that anyone there knew of.
22475	He also gave him a horse,
	and such a one that anyone could say,
	he was the best-mounted man there.
	The ensign of honor was assured him.
	In this way, indeed, he served
22480	the Bishop for a full year,
	except that whenever he turned his hand to gambling,
	the Devil didn't let him lose
	much, for he instructed him,
	turning the dice
22485	skillfully to his profit,
	without anyone knowing it.
	In this way the scholar
	easily won
	all that he wanted,
22490	for the Devil helped him.

Daz treip er wol ein jâr.
der schrîber wart dem bischof gar
liep sicherlîche;
er macht in rîche.
22495 dô er sînen muot erkant,
ze Rôm er in dem bâbst sant
mit einer frömden botschaft.
er gap im zerung die kraft.
des was der schrîbær gemeit.
22500 zuo dem bâbest er dô reit
und warp sîn botschaft als ein man,
der kranken muot nie gewan.
dâ von wart er dem bischof liep.
'er müest sîn ein übel diep,
22505 der mich von dir wolt scheiden.
kristen, juden noch heiden
mac mich von dir gescheiden niht.
diu sæld muoz mit dir haben pfliht.'
alsô sprach der bischof guot:
22510 'ich trag dir holden muot.'
    Ze einen zîten daz geschach,
daz der bischof zuo dem schrîber sprach,
er solt balt ze Rôm varn
und solt sich dar zuo bewarn.
22515 dâ mit der schrîber niht enliez,
swaz in der bischof tuon hiez.
er was im gar bereit.
er fuor ze Rôm mit stætikeit.
als er ûf dem weg reit
22520 wol fünf tagweid, als man seit,
dô kom ein bot und seit mær,
daz der bischof tôt wær;
daz seit man im sicherlîch.
dô sprach der bâbst rîch:
22525 'schrîber, lieber friunt mîn,
dû solt selber bischof sîn.'
zehant er im daz bistuom liez.
vil wol er im dar zuo gehiez,
als dem bâbst der tiufel riet,
22530 wan er in vil gern hiet.
    Dô der schrîber bischof wart,
dô wart niht lenger gespart,

He did this for a good year.
The Bishop had become truly
fond of the scribe;
he made him powerful.
22495 When he recognized his ambition,
he sent him to Rome to the Pope
with a secret message.
He gave him plenty of money for food.
The clerk was pleased about this.
22500 He rode to the Pope
and delivered the message like a man
who has never known despondency.
For this reason, the Bishop was pleased with him.
"That would have to be a wicked thief
22505 who would separate me from you.
Neither Christian, Jew nor Heathen
can separate me from you.
May you be filled with joy."
Thus spoke the good Bishop:
22510 "You are in my favor."
One time it happened
that the Bishop said to the clerk
he should hurry to Rome
and should take good care of himself.
22515 The clerk did not fail,
to do what the Bishop had asked.
He was very willing.
Reliably, he traveled to Rome.
While he was on his way,
22520 a good five days' journey, it is said,
a messenger came and announced
that the Bishop was dead;
he was told this for a fact.
Then the mighty Pope said:
22525 "Clerk, my dear friend,
you yourself shall be Bishop."
At once he gave him the diocese.
And he promised him much more,
at the Devil's instigation,
22530 for he liked him a lot.
When the clerk had become Bishop,
he wasted no more time,

er liebt sich den besten.
kunden unde gesten
22535 gap er sîn brôt willeclîch.
sîn muot der wart freudenrîch.
dô er daz treip driu jâr,
dô starp der bâbst, daz ist wâr.
dô viel diu wal gar an in,
22540 daz dûht den tiufel ein gewin,
wan er ze allen zîten riet,
wan er den schrîber gern hiet.
patriarken und kardinâl
und die fürsten, die die wal
22545 hêten gemein,
die lobten in ein,
daz er bâbest wurde.
daz wart im ein burde.
dô wart niht lenger gespart,
22550 der bischof ze bâbst wart.
do besaz er den stuol schôn,
daz was des tiufels lôn.
  Dar nâch giengen eines tages für in
und sprâchen mit guotem sin
22555 sîn kappellân gemeine:
'herr guot und reine,
ez ist morgen daz reht dîn,
daz dû ze Jerusalêm solt sîn
und solt daz ampt dâ begên,
22560 vil schôn ob dînem alter stên.'
dô daz der bâbst erhôrt und sach,
wider die kapplân er dô sprach:
'wie sol daz immer an mir ergên?
nû muoz doch Jerusalêm stên
22565 enhalb mers. ich muoz verzagen!
wie sol ich in sô kurzen tagen
die kirchen dâ besingen?
wie möht mir sô wol gelingen,
daz ich möht in tag und in naht
22570 über mer, als ir habt gedâht?'
dô sprâchen die kapplân:
'herr, ez mac alsô niht ergân.
ez ist ein kirch hie nâhen bî,

but ingratiated himself with the top people.
He gladly shared his bread
22535 with acquaintances and with strangers.
He was full of the joys.
When he had done this for three years,
the Pope died—that is true.
Then the choice fell upon him;
22540 the Devil saw great profit in this,
for he advised him at all times,
for he liked the clerk.
Patriarchs, cardinals
and princes, who together
22545 had the right to vote,
all agreed
that he should be Pope.
That would be his downfall.
No more time was wasted,
22550 the Bishop became Pope.
Now he possessed the precious throne,
which was the Devil's reward.
      Then one day, all his chaplains
came before him
22555 and said, with no ill intention:
"Good and pure lord,
tomorrow it is your duty,
to go to Jerusalem
and read the office there,
22560 standing at your altar."
When the Pope heard and saw this,
he said to the chaplains:
"How can this happen to me?
For after all, Jerusalem lies
22565 beyond the sea. I can't do this!
How should I sing the mass
in the churches there in so few days?
How could I possibly manage,
to be across the sea, as you suggest,
22570 in just a day and a night?"
At this the chaplains said:
"Lord, that's not the way it is.
There is a church near here,

dâ solt dû morgen sorgen frî
22575   inne singen, daz muoz ergên,
des mac dhein bâbst ab gestên.
diu kirch Jerusalêm ist genant
und ist vil wîten erkant.'
der bâbst gedâht: hôch geborn!
22580   sô ist mîn sêl, mîn lîp verlorn.
     Alsô diu sorg mit im ranc,
unz daz der morgen ûf dranc.
doch muost er mit den kardinâl
varn, daz im daz herz erhal.
22585   er gedâht: ich muoz varn dar!
gegen berg sô gie im daz hâr,
unz er kom ze Jerusalêm geriten.
zehant dô wart niht vermiten,
er gerwet sich an, sicherlîch,
22590   alsam ein bâbest rîch,
sam er daz ampt solt begân.
dô gienc er ûf den letter stân.
er sprach zuo vier knappen sîn:
'iuwer triu sol an mir werden schîn;
22595   ich hân iu hie getrouwet wol.
ir habet mîn red hie für vol.
swer mir iur ieglîcher einen eit
hie vor diser kristenheit,
daz ich iuch heiz schaffen
22600   mit leien und mit pfaffen,
daz ir daz tuot ân widerstrît
hie bî mir an diser zît.'
die knappen sprâchen alle vier:
'herr, ir sult gelouben mir,
22605   wir schaffen hie gern iuwer dinc.'
do sprach under in ein junglinc:
'daz uns niht gêt an daz leben,
daz süln wir nimmer wider streben.'
dâ swuoren si vil schiere
22610   starker eid viere.
dô der bâbst vernam ir eit—
den swuorn si bî ir wârheit—,
er sprach: 'nu bringet einen stoc her,
daz ist mînes herzen ger.

in which you will sing tomorrow
22575   with no difficulty; this must be,
no Pope may refuse this.
The church is called Jerusalem
and is known far and wide."
The Pope thought: "Good Lord!
22580   Then my soul, my life, is lost!"
        He was greatly tormented by worry,
until the next day came.
Yet he had to go with the cardinals,
though his heart was pounding.
22585   He thought: "I have to go!"
His hair stood on end,
all the way to Jerusalem.
Then (there was no avoiding it)
he robed himself
22590   like a mighty Pope
about to read the office.
Then he went and stood at the choir screen.
He said to his four squires:
"Now your faithfulness to me will be tested;
22595   I have trusted you well,
and you have believed in me.
Each of you, swear me an oath
here before these Christian people,
before laity and clergy,
22600   to do what I will now command you,
without arguing,
here at once in my presence."
All four squires said:
"Lord, believe me,
22605   we will gladly do what you require."
Then one of the young men said:
"If it doesn't cost us our lives,
we will never resist it."
On the spot they swore
22610   four binding oaths.
When the Pope heard their oaths
which they swore by their word of honor
he said: "Now bring a block of wood here,
that is the desire of my heart.

22615 dâ bî sô sol ein bîl sîn,
       daz niht scharfer müg gesîn,
       und ein vil starkez mezzer,
       daz nimmer möht sîn bezzer.'
            Dô man daz allez dar brâht,
22620 'ich sag iu, wes ich hân gedâht,'
       sprach der bâbest zehant.
       'lieben liut, sît an mich gemant!
       ich wil mich bîhten offenbâr
       vor diser kristenheit für wâr,
22625 unde daz ir wizzet drât,
       wie mich der tiufel hât
       betrogen als ein krankez wîp:
       ich lobt im sêl unde lîp,
       daz er mich bâbst machet hie.
22630 alsô er mit mir umbegie,
       daz ez ist hie von im geschehen,
       des wil ich vor iu allen jehen.
       hiut sol er mich füeren hin.
       nû hân ich noch zuo got den sin,
22635 daz er sich erbarm über die getât,
       die mîn lîp begangen hât.'
       er sagt in reht, als ez geschach,
       und als der tiufel gegen im jach.
       dar nâch hiez er dar gân
22640 die vier knappen wol getân.
       er sprach: 'slaht mir die füez hin,
       die truogen mich zuo dem tiufel hin.'
       daz wart schier dâ getân.
       er sprach: 'ich wil die hende lân,
22645 dâ mit ich im geschriben hân,
       dem selben tiufelschen man.'
       dar nâch seit er in mit guotem sin:
       'snîdet mir diu ôren hin,
       dâ mit hân ich gehœret in;
22650 des muoz zergên mîn lîp, mîn sin.
       mîn nas muoz daz lîden:
       si wolt des niht vermîden,
       si wolt den tiufel smeckend sîn.
       sô stich mir ûz diu ougen mîn,
22655 diu kunden in vil reht spehen,
       wan si in habent an gesehen.

22615	and with it bring an axe,
	as sharp a one as possible,
	and a very strong knife,
	the best you can get."
	When all this had been brought,
22620	the Pope said at once:
	"I will tell you my intention.
	Good people, take me as a warning!
	I wish to make a public confession
	before this Christian congregation,
22625	and I want you to know here and now,
	how the Devil has tricked me
	as though I were a silly woman:
	I promised him my soul and my life,
	if he would make me Pope here.
22630	His dealings with me were such
	that that has indeed happened,
	I declare this before you all.
	Today he is to come and take me.
	And yet, my thoughts are of God,
22635	that he might have mercy for this thing
	which I have done."
	He told them plainly what had happened,
	and what the Devil had said to him.
	Then he told his four fine squires
22640	to come forward.
	He said: "Chop off my feet,
	they took me to the Devil."
	This was duly done.
	He said: "I want to be parted from my hands,
22645	with which I signed myself over to him,
	that same Devilish being."
	Then he said to them wisely:
	"Cut off my ears,
	with them I listened to him;
22650	therefore my body, my mind, must die.
	Let my nose suffer the same:
	it was not content
	until it had smelt the Devil.
	Then gouge out my eyes,
22655	they were able to see him well,
	for they have looked upon him.

sô ist daz mînes herzen ger,
daz man mir ûz dem rachen her
snîd mîn fleischlîch zunge:
22660 diu hât ir ordnunge
zebrochen, wan si mit im ret,
dâ von si ez güetlîch tet.'
er sprach mit guotem sin:
'werft ez alz den tiufeln hin,
22665 daz si ez in ir rîche
füern gewalticlîche.'
            Den tiufeln ez geworfen wart.
dô wart niht lenger gespart,
si spilten da mit des bales schôn
22670 und hêten in diu kleinet ze lôn.
daz sâhen alle die gemein
in der kirchen, grôz und klein,
die dar komen wâren
bî den selben jâren.
22675 wie ez got mit im schuof dort,
des ist noch nieman an ein ort
komen, an ein wârheit,
wan ez nieman her wider seit.

(26551–26676)

            Ich kan iu wærlîch niht verdagen,
von einem künig wil ich iu sagen,
der was geheizen Salatîn.
zwâr der kund niht milter gesîn:
26555 er gap ros und gewant,
sô man si best veil vant.
silber, golt, edel gestein
gap er allez gemein.
sîn milt sich niht vor êren spielt,
26560 wan er niur einen tische behielt.
der was ein safir grôz,
daz nieman vant sînen genôz,
bezzer dann ein rubîn.
dhein hort kund niht bezzer sîn
26565 wan der selb tisch was.
sîn leng ich geschriben las:
er was drîer ellen lanc.

Then it is the desire of my heart,
that my fleshy tongue
be cut from my jaws:
22660   it offended against propriety
for it spoke with him,
and did so willingly."
He said wisely:
"Throw it all to the Devils,
22665   that they may take it
violently to their realm."
It was thrown to the Devils.
They wasted no time,
but played fine ball games with them
22670   and had these treasures as their reward.
All who were present in the church,
old and young, saw it,
all who had come there
that year.
22675   How God dealt with him then,
no one has ever learned
the truth of it for certain,
for it is not in the record.

[SALADIN'S TABLE]

I really cannot keep this from you:
I want to tell you about a King,
whose name was Saladin.
Truly he could not have been more generous:[14]
26555   he gave stallions, and robes,
the best that could be found on sale.
Silver, gold and gemstones,
all of these he gave.
His generosity was not feigned for the sake of honor,
26560   for he kept only one table for himself.
It was made of a gigantic sapphire,
the likes of which no one had ever seen,
more valuable than a ruby.
No treasure could be better
26565   than this same table was.
I have seen its length written:
it was three cubits long.

zuo dem tisch was manic gedranc
dô man in für den fürsten truoc
26570 sô hêt er schouwær genuoc.
sîn wît wil ich iu mezzen,
des mac ich niht vergezzen,
wan er was an der selben zît
wol zweier dûmellen wît.
26575 sîn tischgestell was von golt,
als ez got wünschen solt.
sô rîchen nieman gesach,
als es manic fürst jach.
swer disen tisch, den stein erkant,
26580 er sprach: 'ich næm in für ein lant.'
    Der herr was milt, als man im jach;
sô miltez herz nieman sach,
sô er hêt in dem lîb sîn,
und tet daz mit werken schîn,
26585 wan vor milt im niht beleip.
den hort er allen von im treip.
ich sag iu allen sîn gelt,
daz er in steten und in velt
hêt vil sicherlîche,
26590 der edel künic rîche,
zehen tûsent unz goldes rôt.
dâ bî leit er grôz nôt
und gebresten von der miltikeit,
wan grôzer gâb was er bereit:
26595 er verseit sîn gâb nieman,
für wâr ich iu daz sagen kan.
sîn gâb er milteclîch tet,
nieman verzêch er sîner bet,
wan milter herz wart nie gesehen,
26600 des muoz ich von schulden jehen.
    Swie milt der selb herr was,
doch wart er siech und niht genas.
dô im diu krancheit wart bekant,
nâch guoten meistern er dô sant
26605 und hiez si sînen brunnen sehen.
si begunden all jehen,
daz er sicher niht möht genesen,
er müest wærlîch tôt wesen.

There was a lot of pushing and shoving when the table
was brought out before the Prince,
26570   as everyone wanted to see it.
I want to tell you its width,
I can't forget that,
for it was also
a good two cubits wide.
26575   It was set in a frame of gold,
as if God himself had perfected it.
No one had ever seen such a splendid one,
as many a prince declared.
Whoever saw this table, the stone,
26580   said: "I would give a whole country for it."
        The gentleman was generous, so they say;
no one ever saw such a generous heart
as he had in his breast,
and this showed itself in action,
26585   for he was so generous that he had nothing left.
He distributed his whole treasure.
I will tell you for a fact
how much money he had
in his towns and in his fields,
26590   this noble and mighty King:
10,000 ounces of gold.
This caused him great distress
and he was bursting with generosity,
for he was ready to make great gifts.
26595   He denied no one a gift,
I can tell you that for a fact.
He gave generously,
he refused no one a request,
for a more generous heart was never seen,
26600   I am obliged to say so.
        As generous as this gentleman was,
he fell sick and did not recover.
When he became aware of his illness,
he sent for the best doctors
26605   and had them check a urine sample.
They all declared
that he certainly could not recover,
and would definitely die.

dô wart er alsô sêr gekleit:
26610 frouwen, ritter unde meit
klagten niht eine,
daz volc gar gemeine
hêt umb in ein sölich klagen,
daz ich ez nimmer kan gesagen.
26615 dô der frum heiden
gesach, daz er solt scheiden
von êr unde von guot,
dô wart trûric sîn muot,
wan sîn leben wolt im leiden.
26620 er sprach: 'sol ich nû scheiden,
sô muoz ich verjehen,
wie sol mîner sêl geschehen?
wer sol der pflegend sîn,
so si scheidet von dem lîb mîn?
26625 wer pfliget ir dann dâ ze stet?
sol ich sie dann Machmet
enpfelhen, daz ist der kristen spot,
die jehent, daz ir herr got
sî sterker dann Machmet;
26630 alsô ieglîch kristen ret.
sô ist mir daz wol bekant,
daz die juden zehant
jehent, daz ir got sterker sî.
welher under den drîen mich sorgen frî
26635 macht, dem wil ich mîn sêl lân
und disen zwein ab gestân.
nû ist leider diser strît
under juden, kristen ze aller zît.
die heiden jehent sîn ouch niht.
26640 daz ist ein jæmerlîch geschiht.
ôwê west ich diu mære,
welher der tiurst wære,
dem wolt ich mînen tisch geben
ân aller hand widerstreben.
26645 sît ich den rehten niht enwizzen kan
und ich ir aller zwîfel hân,
sô wil ich den edeln stein
in teilen gemein,
ich mein den tisch der dâ ist mîn;

Then he was sorely lamented:
26610   ladies, knights and maids
lamented together,
the whole population in chorus
lamented for him so utterly
that I cannot put it into words.
26615   When the pious heathen
saw that he would have to leave
his honor and his wealth,
his heart was sad,
for he was dissatisfied with his life.
26620   He said: "If I must now depart,
I must ask
what will happen to my soul?
Who will take care of it
when it departs from my body?
26625   Who will take care of it then?
If I entrust it to Mohammed,
the Christians will mock;
they say that their Lord God
is stronger than Mohammed;
26630   that's how all the Christians talk.
And I know full well,
that the Jews are quick to say
that their God is stronger.
Whichever of the three will free me
26635   of this worry, to him will I entrust my soul,
distancing myself from the other two.
But unfortunately there is this never-ending
dispute between Jews and Christians.
Nor do the Heathen settle the matter.[15]
26640   This is a sorry state of affairs.
If only I knew for sure,
which of them is the best,
to that God would I give my table
without a moment's hesitation.
26645   Since I cannot know which is right
and I mistrust all of them,
I shall divide that whole
gemstone between them,
—I mean that table of mine;

26650   zwâr der muoz ir drîer sîn.'
        den tisch hiez er für sich tragen.
        daz kan ich iu für wâr sagen,
        ein bîl dâ bereitet wart.
        dô wart niht lenger gespart,
26655   den tisch hiez er mit heil
        teilen in driu teil.
        daz ein teil gap er ze stet
        sînem got Machmet,
        daz ander teil ân spot
26660   gap er durch der kristen got:
        daz dritt teil gap er gar
        für der juden got zwâr.
        er sprach: 'swelher sterker sî,
        der muoz mich tuon sorgen frî,
26665   wan ich niht bezzers wizzen kan.'
        alsô sprach der frum man:
        'und sî daz got der heiden
        gewaltic sî, der müez mich scheiden
        von mînem ungemach gar,
26670   swenn mîn sêl von hinnen var;
        sî aber der kristen got
        gewaltic, der helf mir ûz nôt;
        sî aber got der juden rîch
        gewaltic sicherlîch,
26675   der müez mich niht von im verlân.'
        dâ mit diu sêle schiet von dan.

(28003–28036)

        Dô wart der keiser Fridrîch
        erwelt schôn sicherlîch
28005   und wart gewaltic, als man seit,
        daz er den bâbst ûz Rôm treip,
        bischof und kardinâl:
        die fluhen all über al.
        dô er dô gewaltic wart,
28010   dô huop er sich an die vart
        und underwant sich der land
        vil gar ân alle schand.
        nû weiz ich niht, wie ez kam,

26650 In truth, there will have to be three of them."
 He had the table brought before him.
 And I can tell you the truth of the matter:
 an axe was prepared.
 No more time was wasted,
26655 he had the table neatly split
 into three parts.
 At once he gave one part
 to his God Mohammed,
 the second part—honestly!—
26660 he gave to the Christians' God:
 the third part in truth he gave
 to the God of the Jews.
 He said: "Whichever of them is strongest,
 let him take away my worries,
26665 for I cannot know better than that."
 Thus spoke the righteous man:
 "And if the Heathens' God
 reigns, let him relieve me
 of all my distress,
26670 when my soul departs from here;
 but if the Christians' God
 reigns, let him help me in my crisis;
 but if in fact the mighty God
 of the Jews reigns,
26675 let him not reject me."
 With that, his soul departed.

[THE FIRST EXCOMMUNICATION OF FREDERICK II][16]

 Thus the Emperor Frederick
 was indeed elected
28005 and became so powerful, it is said,
 that he drove the Pope from Rome;
 bishops and cardinals
 fled in all directions.
 When he had gained in strength,
28010 he mounted a campaign
 and subjugated the entire land,
 without any loss to his own honor.
 Now I don't know how it came about

daz in der bâbst in sîn æht nam
28015   unde tet in in den ban,
dar zuo all sîn man.
doch wart mir daz bekant,
der kriec wær umb Zeciljenlant.
daz wolt der bâbst gern hân;
28020   des wolt der keiser im niht lân.
dâ von huop sich der strît.
si hêten beidenthalben nît.
zwâr umb daz selb lant
huop sich roup unde brant.
28025   dar nâch hêt er wîten sweif:
swâ er des bâbstes liut begreif,
die hiez er mit nœten
wærlîch all tœten.
die pfaffen muosten dô irn sweiz
28030   lâzen, wan er in ûz reiz
die platen ûz dem houbt her.
daz was sînes herzen ger.
die bruoder mohten im niht enpfliehen,
er hiez in ab ziehen
28035   die hût über diu ôren
als si wæren tôren.

(28037–28104)

Nû merket, keiser Fridrîch,
des frümkeit was niht gelîch—
wan unzuht muost in vliehen—,
28040   er hiez stecher ziehen:
an swem er sich wolt rechen,
den hiez er wærlîch stechen.
der ein fürst was genant,
dem hiez er tuon den tôt bekant.
28045   die arm hiez er mit nœten
wærlîch all tœten,
swer den tôt hêt verscholt;
dâ für nam er dhein golt.
swelich kint hêt zwei jâr,
28050   diu hiez er wærlîchen zwâr
under die erden lâzen.

	that the Pope excommunicated him,
28015	placing him under the ban of the Church,
	together with all his vassals.
	But I do know that the issue
	of the war was Sicily:
	the Pope wanted control of it
28020	but the Emperor wouldn't give it up to him.
	That was the source of the conflict.
	There was great enmity on both sides.
	Truly, pillage and arson[17]
	engulfed the whole land.
28025	His power reached far and wide:
	wherever he caught adherents of the Pope,
	in truth, he gave the command
	that they all suffer a painful death.
	The blood of the priests was shed
28030	when he ripped
	the tonsure from their heads.
	This was the desire of his heart.
	The monks could not flee him.
	He had their skin
28035	pulled over their ears
	as though they were fools.

[FREDERICK AND THE ASSASSINS]

	Now hear of the Emperor Frederick,
	whose virtue was second to none
	(for impropriety was unknown to him):
28040	he commanded that assassins be raised.
	Whenever he wanted to be avenged on anyone
	he had them stabbed.
	Whoever had the title of Prince,
	he ordered that he be made acquainted with death.
28045	In truth, he gave the command
	that the poor should all suffer a painful death
	as many of them as had earned death;
	he took no gold as a bribe instead.
	Whenever a child reached the age of two
28050	he commanded—this is true—
	that he be confined underground.

er lie si niht zuo den strâzen.
er verbôt daz man in dhein lieht
gæb noch in nimmer niht
28055　den tac liez schouwen an.
swer mit in solt umbe gân,
dem gebôt er mit kündikeit,
daz er den kinden iht enseit
wan daz er got wære.
28060　dô si erhôrten diu mære,
dô wânten si, im wær alsô,
er wær got von himel dô,
sô er die boten zuo in sant;
diu wârheit was in unbekant.
28065　sô diu kint wurden alt,
sô seite man vil manicvalt
wunder daz hie ûz geschæch.
'ô wê! wie gern ich daz sæch,'
sprach ieglîchez kindelîn.
28070　'ich muoz hie inn verslozzen sîn.'
sô dann der keiser Fridrîch
wolt stechen einen fürsten rîch,
sô hiez er zwei kint zehant
ledic lâzen ûz dem bant.

man furte si in einen garten,
danne man freude mocht warten.
do waren zarte junfrowen inne,
di sach man mangerlei beginne:
5　er enteil di sungen,
daz ander teil di sprungen.
di derten di worffen den bal.
si hatten freude ober al.
di junfrowen waren wol getan.
10　si hatten riche cleider an
von siden und von baldekin.
si musten ouch schone bespenget sin.
do waren ouch schoner frowen gnug.
riche koste man dare trug,
15　daz der di kinder ouch geszen
in schonen gulden gefeszen.

He did not let them out on the streets.
He forbade them to be given
light, nor ever
28055   to be allowed to see day.
He cunningly commanded all those
who had to deal with them
to tell the children nothing other
than that he was God.
28060   When they heard these reports
they believed it was true
that he was God from Heaven above,
when he sent his messengers to them;
the truth was unknown to them.
28065   When the children grew up
they were told many wondrous things
of the world outside.
"Alas! How I would like to see that,"
said each of the little children,
28070   "I have to stay locked up in here."
Then when the Emperor Frederick
wanted to assassinate a powerful Prince,
he at once had two children
released from their imprisonment.

They were led into a garden[18]
which promised great pleasures.
It was full of attractive maidens
who could be seen doing many things.
5   One group were singing,
the second were dancing,
the third playing ball—
they had pleasures finer than any others.
The virgins were beautiful;
10   they wore ornate clothes
of silk and of brocade,
and had beautiful spangles on—
beautiful ladies were not in short supply.
Rich food was carried in,
15   so that the children might eat of it
in fine golden dishes.

si hatten vorre geszen dort
nicht danne waszer und brot
bi alle eren jaren,
20   do si an deme dinstern waren.
man schankete en ouch do yn
beide mete und win;
uf daz si di trenke gesmeckten,
man liez si wenig darane lecken.
25   keiser Frederich der quam danne gegan,
der hatte schone cleider an,
und alle di mit eme gingen,
di horte man ferre clingen,
also ez were frou Holde,
30   von silber und von golde.
spellute waren ouch do gnug.
iclicher sine zirde trug,
also her schonest werde mochte,
und allez daz zu freuden tochte,
35   daz brachte man allez dar,
daz sin di kinder worden gewar.
do hub sich schrecken und tucken,
beide phiffen und pucken,
bosunen und schalmeyen.
40   so gingen si danne an eynen reien.
do was danne freude unmaszen vel
und mannig gut seiten spel.

28075   sô si dann sâhen die wunne,
daz diu lûter sunne
schein alsô liehtgevar,
und si der waid nâmen war,

und di blumen und daz grune gras
und des bornes der in deme garten was,
der boime und die fruchte
und der schonen junfrowen zuchte
5   und der vogelin gesang:
di wile duchte si nicht lang,
und horten di spel irclingen
und di lute in freuden springen.

Prior to this they had eaten
nothing but bread and water
through all their years
20   when they had lived in the dark.
Now both mead and wine
were poured out for them;
in order that they might taste these drinks
they were allowed to sip a little from them.
25   The Emperor Frederick now appeared,
wearing fine clothes,
as did all who were with him,
clothes which could be heard from a distance,
jingling with silver and gold,[19]
30   as though it were Hulda.
There were many musicians there too,
each fully adorned
as beautifully as he could,
and everything which brings pleasure
35   was brought out
for the children to see.
Then began the shrill and lively sound
of pipes and drums,
trumpet and shawm.
40   Then they danced in a ring.
Then there was joy beyond all bounds—
and fine music from the strings.

28075   When they now saw the splendor
of the radiant sun
which shone so brightly,
and when they saw the meadows,[20]

and the flowers, and the green grass,
and the stream which flowed through the garden,
the trees and the fruit
and the refinement of the fair maidens,
5   and the song of the birds,
(they were completely enchanted)
and heard the music
and the people dancing with joy,

28080
dô sprâchen si: 'herr guot,
wir biten iuch, daz ir sô wol tuot
und uns lât hie belîben,
mit iu die zît vertrîben.
wir haben sô schœnez nie gesehen,
des müezen wir wærlîchen jehen,

28085
wan iu ist niht gelîche
in iuwerm himelrîche.'
dô sprach der keiser zehant:
'gebt mir iuwer triu ze pfant,
daz ir tuot swaz ich wil,

28090
sô wil ich iuch der freuden zil
lâzen wærlîchen von mir spehen.
ich lâz iuch manic wunder sehen.'
sô dann die stechære
erhôrten diu mære,

28095
sô sprâchens: 'lieber herr guot,
wir biten iuch daz ir sô wol tuot,
daz ir uns lât vor iu gân.'
'allez daz ieman gesprechen kan,
dâ mit ich iu gedienen mac,

28100
daz sûm ich nimmer einen tac.'
und ir dheiner daz enliez,
swen der keiser stechen hiez,
den stach der stecher an der stat,
swenn in der keiser stechen bat.

(28105–28204)

28105
Ze einen zîten daz geschach,
als man mir von im verjach,
daz er drî man hêt gefangen,
di solden alle drî hangen,
wan si ez hêten wol verscholt.

28110
er was in vînt und niht holt.
zuo einen zîten daz geschach,
der keiser wider die herren jach,
wan er saz nicht eine.
dô trahten die herren gemeine,

28115
wer aller best möht verdeuwen,
des sich die arzât möhten freuwen.

they said, "Good Lord,
28080   we beseech you to be so gracious
as to let us remain here
and spend our time with you.
We have never seen anything so beautiful,
truly we have to say this,
28085   for there is no one like you
in your Heaven."
Then the Emperor said at once
"Give me your pledge
that you will do whatever I ask,
28090   then in truth I will let you
see joy in all its fullness.
I will show you many wonders."
When the assassins
heard these words
28095   they said: "Dear good Lord,
we beseech you to be so gracious
as to let us remain in your presence.
Anything which anyone can name
by which I can serve you,
28100   I will not hesitate for a moment."
And none of them refused.
When the Emperor ordered someone to be killed,
the assassin killed him at once,
as soon as the Emperor asked him to do it.

[A MEDICAL EXPERIMENT]

28105   Once it happened,
so the story goes,
that he had three prisoners
who were all to be hanged,
for they had all quite deserved it.
28110   He was angry with them, and not conciliatory.
One day
the Emperor was speaking with his nobles,
for he did not hold court alone.
The nobles were discussing amongst themselves
28115   who had the best digestion,
to the doctors' satisfaction.

dô sprach zehant ein arzât:
'nieman sô wol verdeuwet hât
sô ein slâfender man,
28120 für wâr ich iu daz sagen kan.'
der ander sprach zwâr,
verdeut hiet nieman sô gar
sô der ein pfert rennen sol:
'daz weiz ich von der wârheit wol.'
28125 der dritt sprach an der stat:
'ir sült mir gelouben drât,
daz nieman sô schier verdeuwet hât
sô der loufet unde gât.'
dô sprach der keiser Fridrîch:
28130 'daz wil ich sehen sicherlîch.
ich hân drî gevangen;
die solden billîch hangen,
wan ich lâz si niht genesen.
swer bî der kunst wil wesen,
28135 der sol über die siben tag
zwâr nâch des buoches sag
die wârheit hie kiesen.
den lîp si müezen verliesen.
ich muoz besehen die wârheit,
28140 welich arzt hab reht geseit.
daz wil ich wærlîch sehen,
welhem ich der kunst müg verjehen.'
zehant hiez er die drî man
all drî ungezzen lân
28145 zwâr unz an den dritten tac.
daz was in dô ein grôzer slac.
dar nâch hiez er in geben spîs:
si was gesoten in der wîs,
daz ez in übel gezam:
28150 rôhez man ez von den heven nam.
doch hêten si den hunger starc:
si nâmen ez für zehen marc
unde dar zuo für vier.
gâz hêten si ez schier.
28155 zehant man in mêr für truoc,
unz si gâzen genuoc.
dem einen gap man trinkens vil,
des ich iu niht helen wil.

At once one doctor spoke up:
"No one has better digestion
than a man who is asleep,
28120   that I can tell you!"
Then, sure enough, the second spoke:
"No one has ever digested as well
as when he was riding a horse,
I know that for a fact!"
28125   At once a third spoke up:
"You can take my word for it:
no one has digested so quickly
as when he was running and walking."
Then the Emperor Frederick said:
28130   "I want to know the truth of this matter.
I have three prisoners
who should by rights be hanged,
for I do not intend to pardon them.
Whoever wishes to know the result,
28135   in one week from today . . ."
—so the book tells us—[21]
". . . will perceive the truth.
These three men must die;
I must see for certain
28140   which doctor has spoken correctly.
Indeed I want to discover
which doctor I should praise for his skill."
At once he ordered that the three men
should all be left without food
28145   until the third day.
That came as a shock to them!
After that he ordered that they be given food.
It had been boiled in a manner
which made it quite unpalatable for them:
28150   it was still raw when it was taken from the pots.
Yet they were extremely hungry
and would have taken it if it had cost them ten marks
or even fourteen,
they would still have eaten it quickly.
28155   At once they were given more
until they had had all they could eat.
One of them was given a lot to drink,
I will make no secret of that.

twalm man im în gôz,
28160   daz er im in den lîp flôz.
dô leit er sich als ein man
der nie âtem gewan.
alsô lac er drî tag
nâch des buoches sag.
28165   den andern man loufen bat
unz ze Bern in die stat,
daz man in niht liez rasten;
mit geiseln und mit asten
bert man im den ruck sîn,
28170   daz diu fluht wart an im schîn.
zwâr man im den rucken bert:
nieman ez den Walhen wert.
dô im entweich kraft und maht,
mit slegen man in dar zuo brâht,
28175   daz er muost aber loufen.
von slegen und von roufen
gewan er angst unde nôt,
daz er lac ûf dem veld tôt.
den dritten man dô rennen hiez,
28180   wan man in des niht erliez,
er müest rennen ze aller zît
daz velt nâhen unde wît.
swann sin pfert müed wart,
sô wart niht lenger gespart,
28185   man bræht im ein anderz drât.
des wolt man niht haben rât,
er müest rennen ze stunt,
unz im der tôt wart kunt.
dô der keiser Fridrîch
28190   hiez die tôten snîden gelîch,
welhem tôten man des jach,
dô man ieslîchs spîs sach,
welich aller best wær verdeuwet.
dô wart der arzt gefreuwet,
28195   der dô den slâfunden man
hêt der dô den sic gewan,
wan er hêt aller best verdeuwet.
der selbe arzt sich des freuwet.

	A sedative was mixed into it
28160	so that it flowed down into his body.
	At this he collapsed, like a man
	who had never drawn breath.
	Thus he lay for three days—
	so the book tells us.
28165	The second man was made to run
	all the way to the city of Verona,[22]
	and was not allowed to rest.
	With whips and with rods
	they flayed his back
28170	so that he fled from them.
	They flayed his back thoroughly
	and no one stopped those Italians.[23]
	Whenever he ran out of strength and power,
	their blows induced him
28175	to start running again.
	The blows and the beatings
	caused him such fear and distress
	that he lay dead on the ground.
	The third man was ordered to go riding,
28180	for there was no respite for him.
	He had to ride continuously
	near and far across the plains.
	Whenever his horse became tired
	no time was wasted,
28185	they brought him another one at once.
	Nothing would do, but that
	he should ride and ride
	until he became acquainted with death.
	Then the Emperor Frederick
28190	had the dead men slit open at once,
	to discover which of them
	would be declared to have digested best,
	when all of their food had been seen.
	Satisfaction fell to the doctor
28195	who had tipped on the sleeping man.
	He won the argument,
	for this man had digested best,
	much to the satisfaction of that doctor.

              Dannoch der keiser niht enlie,
28200   manic wunder er begie.
              nâch maniger hand dingen,
              nâch witzen begund er ringen.
              des gewan er vünt genuoc.
              er wart an mangen dingen kluoc.

(28205–28532)

28205   Der keiser einen gesellen hêt,
              dem elliu frümkeit wol an stêt.
              von Antfurt her Fridrîch,
              alsô was sîn nam rîch.
              er was der höbschist man,
28210   den al diu werlt geleisten kan.
              er hêt erworben manic wîp,
              den gezieret was ir lîp.
              ze jungst sazt er sîn sinne
              an ein edle grævinne.
28215   diu was sô schœn, als man seit,
              daz in sîn muot dick jeit
              unde all sîn sinne
              nâch der edeln grævinne.
              dô wolt daz schœn wîp
28220   mit im niht teilen irn lîp.
              si sprach zuo im: 'her Fridrîch,
              ir sült daz wizzen sicherlîch,
              lât ir mich niht mit frid sîn,
              ich sag ez dem herren mîn.'
28225   er sprach: 'swie ez mir sol ergân,
              von iu sô mac ich niht enlân,
              mir werd dann iuwer minne
              oder ich verlur mîn sinne.'
              daz treip er mit ir, daz ist wâr,
28230   mêr dann driu jâr.
              do gedâht si in irem muot:
              'ei! milter got vil guot,
              wie tæt ich disem ritter guot,
              daz er von mir liez sînen muot?
28235   ich kan in niht erwenden,
              er well mir boten senden.

After that the Emperor did not stop,

28200 but did many amazing things.

He pursued many questions,

seeking answers to puzzles,

and thus he made many discoveries.

He became learned in many spheres of knowledge.

[FREDERICK OF ANTFURT AND THE LADY'S CHEMISE][24]

28205 The Emperor had a friend

who was a model of courage.

Frederick of Antfurt

was his high-born name.

Of all the men the world can boast,

28210 he was the most courtly in his conduct.

He had won round many women

of comely appearance.

Finally his attention was caught

by a noble Countess.

28215 She is said to have been so beautiful

that his mood and all his thoughts

often drove him

to seek out the noble Countess.

However the beautiful woman

28220 did not want to sleep with him.

She said to him, "Sir Frederick,

you should be in no doubt

that if you do not leave me in peace

I will tell my lord about it."

28225 He said, "No matter what it cost me,

I can't stop wooing you

unless I win your love,

for otherwise I will go mad."

Indeed, he behaved like this towards her

28230 for more than three years.

Then she thought to herself,

"Oh! Good and gracious God,

what should I do with this good knight

to make him turn his thoughts from me?

28235 I can't persuade him

to stop sending me messengers.

möht ich in mit höbscheit
dar zuo bringen, daz im leit
geschæch von den schulden sîn,
28240   und ich doch niht arne pîn,
alsô daz er mit grôzer nôt
von sînen schulden læg tôt,
daz ich behielt mîn êre!
mich müet daz hart sêre,
28245   daz er niht wil die red lân.
ich wird im nimmer undertân.'
daz wort si weinend sprach
und wider ir herz daz verjach.
vil siuftens in ir herz viel,
28250   wann ir dô der sorgen schiel
von disem ritter wart kunt,
niht eines, zwâr ze manger stunt.
    Dar nâch si ir gedâhte
daz in in kumber brâhte.
28255   'owê! lieber herr mîn,
sol ich in untriun bî dir sîn,
so verlur ich mîn wirdikeit,
wan mir ist al bôsheit leit.
solt ich von dir gescheiden sîn—
28260   ich mein dich, lieber herr mîn,
mit herzen und mit triuwen—,
daz müest mich immer riuwen.'
si meint iren lieben man,
dem si alles guotes gan.
28265   si gedâht: ob mir daz geschæch,
daz man mir der bôsheit jæch
von mînem kranken sinne,
ich wolt ê verbrinnen.
eins tags kom der ritter dar
28270   unde nam ir tougen war
und bat si umb ir minne,
die edeln grævinne.
'her Fridrîch, wolt ir mich gewern
des ich an iuch mac begern?'
28275   dô sprach ez her Fridrîch:
'frou, wizzet sicherlîch,

If only I could use some courtly convention
so that harm may befall him
through his own actions
28240   and without any unpleasantness for me[25]
so that he would fall into great danger
and die through his own actions,
that I might keep my honor!
It troubles me greatly
28245   that he will not stop saying these things.
I will never submit to him."
She spoke these words with tears,
and despite the feelings of her heart.
Her heart was rent with sighs,
28250   for this knight had caused
the splinter of care to pierce it,[26]
not once, but many times.
          Then she considered
what would make trouble for him.
28255   "Alas! My dear lord,
should I be unfaithful to you,
I would lose my honor,
for I hate all evil.
If I should be separated from you,
28260   (for I love you, my dear lord,[27]
with heart and soul),
I would grieve forever."
By this she meant her dear husband,
for whom she wished everything that is good.
28265   She thought, "If it should come about
that I am accused of wrongdoing
through my foolish thoughts,
I would rather burn."
One day the knight came
28270   and saw her secretly,
and asked her, the noble Countess,
for her love.
"Sir Frederick, would you grant me
anything I could ask of you?"
28275   Sir Frederick answered:
"Lady, know for certain,

swaz ir habt in iuwerm muot'—
alsô sprach der ritter guot—,
'daz wil ich niht zerbrechen.
28280 solt man mich ze tôd stechen,
daz wolt ich lîden sicherlîch,'
alsô sprach her Fridrîch;
'und möht ich iuwer huld gehân,
ich wær iu dienstes undertân.'
28285 dô sprach daz minniclîch wîp:
'und sol ich mit iu mînen lîp
teilen, daz müezt ir dienen alsô,
daz ich sîn muoz werden vrô.'
er sprach: 'swaz ir mir vor saget,
28290 daz tuot mîn lîp unverzaget.'
si sprach: 'sich hebt ein turnei
hie in der stat. sô briht enzwei
manic ritter sîn sper,
dem ze ritterschaft ist ger.
28295 mügt ir dann der best sîn,
dô wil ich iu den lîp mîn
mit teilen, als ich iu sagen wil.
mügt ir der sper brechen vil
und dann in einer frouwen kleit
28300 sît ze ritterschaft bereit
gegen einem der harnasch füer,
für wâr ich iu des swüer,
vertuot ir dâ iur scharpfez sper,
iurr bet ich iuch billîch gewer,
28305 und komt ir lebentic von dan.
swie lieb mir ist mîn man,
doch wil ich sicherlîchen
iurn triuwen niht entwîchen.'
dô sprach der frum man:
28310 'frou, ob ichz wol enden kan
mit lîb und mit guote,
daz ist mir wol ze muote.
ich wil den turnei gern holn,
sol ich den tôt von iu doln.'
28315 si sprach: 'und ist, daz ez geschiht,
ich versag iu mîner minn niht.'

whatever it is that is on your mind . . ."
thus spoke the good knight
". . . I will not refuse it.

28280   Even though I were to be run through,
I would certainly accept it . . ."
thus spoke Sir Frederick,
". . . if I could win your favor,
I would submit to your service."

28285   Then the lovely woman said,
"If I am to sleep with you
you must earn it in a way
which pleases me."
He said, "Whatever you ask of me,

28290   that I will do without hesitation."
She said, "There will be a tournament
here in the town. Many a knight
who is intent on knightly combat
will break his lance there.

28295   If you can prove to be the best one among them,
then I promise
I will sleep with you.
If you can break many lances
and then are willing to joust

28300   in a woman's dress
against one who is wearing armor,
truly I swear to you,
if you split your sharp lance then,
I will willingly grant your request,

28305   should you come out of it alive.
As dear as my husband is to me,
yet I will surely
not break trust with you."
At this, the brave man said,

28310   "Lady, if I can achieve this
and keep my life and property,
I will be well pleased.
I will gladly take part in the tournament
even if it means I die for you."

28315   She said, "If you do this,
I will not deny you my love."

      Dô der turnei wart volbrâht,
als ir diu frou hêt gedâht,
dô kom der von Antfurt.
28320   ein sper er degenlîch fuort
gegen einem ritter lobesam,
den er ûz den andern nam.
er sprach: 'welt ir ein sper
mit mir, edler ritter hêr,
28325   vertuon, als ich iu hie sag?
ir sît ein helt und niht ein zag:
dar umb sô bit ich iuch sicherlîch,
daz ir durch iuwer frouwen rîch
ein sper mit mir vertuot hie.
28330   doch wil ich iu sagen, wie:
ir sült gên mir gewâpent sîn:
sô wil ich durch die frouwen mîn
blôz gegen iu rennen.
mîn wâpen sol man erkennen:
28335   daz ist niht wan ein frouwen kleit.
also bin ich zuo der tjost bereit.'
dô sprach der edel ritter guot:
'sô hiet ich einn verzagten muot,
solt ich an füern und ir niht:
28340   daz wær ein zeglîch geschiht.'
dô sprach ez her Fridrîch:
'nein, edler ritter freudenrîch,
lig ich von iuwern handen tôt,
als mir mîn frou hie gebôt,
28345   so vergib ich iu mit triuwen.
mîn tôt iuch niht sol riuwen,
wan ich stirb durch di frouwen mîn.
wie möht mir immer baz gesîn?'
alsô bat er den selben man,
28350   unz er kom zuo im ûf den plân.
ze samen si dô kêrten,
als si ir manheit lêrte.
sîn sper her Fridrîch verstach
vil schôn, als im diu meng jach.
28355   der ander in ouch gevie,
daz daz sper durch in gie
mitten wol einer ellen lanc.

When the tournament had been arranged
as the lady had anticipated,
the knight of Antfurt arrived.
28320 He bore a lance heroically
against a praiseworthy knight
whom he had chosen from among the others.
He said, "Will you split a lance
with me, noble knight,
28325 as I will explain?
You are a hero, and no coward:
therefore I ask you indeed
in the name of your high-born lady,
that you split a lance with me here.
28330 But I will tell you how:
you will come against me in armor,
and I, in my lady's name,
will ride against you unarmored.
You will recognize my armour:
28335 it is nothing but a woman's dress.
On these terms I am ready to joust."
Then the good and noble knight said,
"I would have a cowardly spirit
if I should wear armor and you not.
28340 That would truly be cowardice."
Then Sir Frederick said,
"No, blithe, noble knight,
if I lie dead from your hand
as my lady has commanded it,
28345 then I forgive you completely.
You should not regret my death,
for I die for my lady.
What better thing could befall me?"
Thus he cajoled that same man
28350 until he rode out onto the field against him.
They came against each other
as their manliness required.
Sir Frederick struck well with his lance,
as the watching crowds declared.
28355 His opponent also hit him
so well that his lance went through Frederick,
through his middle, fully an ell's length.[28]

diu unmaht vast mit im ranc,
daz er von dem ross ze tal
28360   hienc und erviel ûf daz wal
unde man in dannen truoc.
umb in wart grôz klag genuoc.
        Merket wie diu grævin sprach,
dô si den ritter ligen sach:
28365   'ôwê, reines mannes muot!
wie hâst dû lîp unde guot
umb mînen lîp gegeben!
dû hâst dîn tugentlîchez leben
durch mînen willen hie verlân.
28370   daz ich dîn künd ie gewan,
daz ist mir hie ein grôz nôt.
dû lîst durch mînen willen tôt.
ôwê, vil sæliger lîp,
möhtest dû dîn dienst an ein wîp
28375   gekêrt hân diu dich hiet gewert!
mîn lîp niht wan mîns herren gert.
dâ von wær dû ein tumber man,
daz dû dîn leben hâst verlân
durch mich, ich bin ein armez wîp:
28380   dû hietest schœnern lîp
gewunnen dann ich bin gewesen;
dâ von dû wærst wol genesen.
des riuwet sicher mich dîn tôt.
dû hâst wærlîch durch mich die nôt
28385   erliten und den smerzen.
ich hêt in mînem herzen
mich des vermezzen:
des möht ich niht vergezzen,
daz mîn lîp dheinem man
28390   wurd nimmer undertân
dann dem lieben herren mîn.
diu stæt muoz immer an mir sîn.'
        Nû wil ich sagen wie im geschach,
als im diu meist meng jach.
28395   dô lac er für wâr
mêr dann ein jâr,
unz der siechtuom von im vlôch.

Unconsciousness overwhelmed him
so that he hung down from his horse
28360   and fell to the ground in the lists,
from where they carried him away.
He was greatly lamented.
        Hear how the Countess spoke,
when she saw the knight lying there.
28365   "Alas, pure spirit of manliness!
That you have laid down life and goods
for the sake of my flesh!
You have lost your
virtuous life at my desire.
28370   How bitterly I now regret
that I ever heard of you.
You lie dead at my desire.
Alas, that fine physique,
if only you could have offered your service to a woman
28375   who would have yielded what you wanted!
My body desires none but my lord's.
This is why you were a foolish man
to leave your life for me.
I am a pitiful woman!
28380   You could have won a prettier figure
than I am,
then you would surely be alive.
So I deeply regret your death.
You have truly suffered this calamity
28385   and this pain because of me.
In my heart
I had boasted of this:
that I couldn't forget
that my body would never be subject
28390   to any man
other than my dear lord.
In this I must remain constant forever."
        Now I shall tell you what happened to him,
as the story is normally told.
28395   Truly, he lay there
for over a year
until the injury left him.

ein rîsen man durch in zôch
unde hært in sam ein ros,
28400   daz wunt ist worden in einem mos.
dô er dô gesunt wart,
dô wart niht lenger gespart,
er gie zuo sîner frouwen guot,
der er dâ truoc holden muot.
28405   mit im er daz hemd truoc—
daz was sweizic genuoc—,
dâ er inn was worden wunt.
er sprach: 'frou, ich bin gesunt.
nû sehet, frou wol getân,
28410   waz ich smerzen erliten hân,
und seht daz an, schœnez wîp,
ob ich iht iuwern schœnen lîp
hab jæmerlîch erarnôt.'
er zeigt ir daz hemdel rôt,
28415   daz er an im fuorte,
do daz sper durch in ruorte.
dô si daz hemdel ersach,
vil bermclîch si wider in sprach:
'nû wizz ez got der rîch,
28420   daz niht sô bitter wær gelîch,
ich wolt ez tuon williclîch,
ê daz ich an mînem herren rîch
mîn triu zerbræch ze dheiner vrist.
möhtet ir iu indert dheinen list
28425   für setzen den ich tæt,
daz ich mîn êr behielt stæt?'
dô sprach der edel ritter guot:
'sît ir habt sô vesten muot
und iuwer êr behaltet gern,
28430   wolt ir mich einer dig gewern,
daz ir, frou wol getân,
wolt tuon als ich iu sagen kan?'
dô sprach si: 'lieber herr mîn,
daz kan sô bitter niht gesîn
28435   noch an mir sô grôz nôt:
daz ich niur niht kies den tôt,
des andern wil ich volgent sîn,
daz ich behalt die triu mîn.'

He had been stitched up with hair-thread,
sewn together like a horse
28400 which has been injured in a bog.
When he had recovered,
he wasted no more time
but went to his good lady,
to whom his heart belonged.
28405 He took with him the chemise
(it was bloody enough!)
in which he had been injured.
He said, "Lady, I am well.
Now see, fair lady,
28410 what pains I have suffered,
and see this, beautiful woman,
how terribly I have earned
your beautiful body."
He showed her the red chemise
28415 which he had been wearing
when the lance ran him through.
When she saw the chemise,
she said to him most pitifully,
"Almighty God knows
28420 that there is nothing so unpalatable
that I wouldn't gladly do it
rather than break trust at any time
with my high-born lord.
Is there no other task
28425 you can set for me,
that I might still keep my honor?"
Then the good and noble knight said,
"Since you are so determined
to keep your honor,
28430 will you grant me one request
which you, fair lady,
will perform as I prescribe it?"
At this she said, "My dear lord,
it can be nothing so awful,
28435 nor cause me such dire straits:
Only, let me not die;
anything else I will obey
if it means I can keep faith."

er sprach: 'ez ist diu hôchzît,
28440 daz man in dem land wît
begêt pfingsten di vîrtag.
nâch mîner lêr sag
sô sült ir anders niht pflegen,
ir sült daz pfeitel an legen,
28445 dâ ich inn wunt worden bin.
nû merket reht mînen sin:
ir sült an sant Steffans tag
nâch mîner lêr sag
an iu daz sweizic hemdel tragen.
28450 noch wil ich iu mêr sagen:
ein rîsen sült ir haben guot,
einen mantel ân huot,
zwên schuoch alsô niuwe.
und welt ir iuwer triuwe
28455 behalten, sô ir ze opfer gêt
unde vor dem alter stêt,
sô lât vallen den mantel guot,
daz ich ez sech, frou wol behuot,
wan ich wil in dem kôr stên,
28460 sô ir sült ze opfer gên.
tuot ir dann, frou wol getân,
als ich iu gesagt hân,
sô sît ir billîch frî,
swie halt mir gelungen sî.'
28465 dô sprach diu frou wol getân:
'swie halt ez mir süll ergân,
ob ez mir wirt ein herzenleit,
swaz ir mir vor habt geseit,
daz wil ich allez leisten gar,
28470 daz sag ich iu für wâr.'
   Dô diu hôchzît kam,
die pfingsten, als ich vernomen hân,
dô nam diu frou daz hemdel rôt,
als ir her Fridrîch gebôt;
28475 einen mantel si dar über swief.
irr junkfroun eine si dô rief,
daz si ir trüeg schuoch und rîsen;
dar în wolt si sich brîsen.

He said, "It is the holy season
28440 which is kept throughout the land,
the feast of Pentecost.[29]
My requirement of you
is nothing other than this,
that you should put on the garment
28445 in which I was injured.
Now listen carefully to what I want:
on St. Stephen's Day
I tell you, you will
wear the blood-stained chemise.
28450 And furthermore,
you will have a good veil,
a gown without a hood,
and a new pair of shoes.
And if you want to keep faith,
28455 when you go to take the sacrament
and stand before the altar,
then drop your fine gown
so I can see it, my oh-so-chaste lady,
for I will be standing in the choir
28460 when you go to the sacrament.
For if, fair lady, you do
what I have told you,
you will be free of your bond
even if I have nothing from it."
28465 At this the fair lady said,
"No matter what becomes of me,
even if it causes me great sorrow,
I will do everything exactly
as you have said it,
28470 I give you my word."
When the holy day arrived
(it was Pentecost, so they say)
the lady took the red chemise
as Sir Frederick had commanded,
28475 and threw a gown over it.
She called one of her maidservants
to fetch her some shoes and a veil,
and in these she wanted to be dressed.

zuo der kirchen si dô gie;
28480　　ir zuht si niht enlie.
dâ stuont si ze kirchen schôn.
ir zuht gap ir der êren krôn.
si wartet des offertorium.
dô man daz sanc, zwên ritter frum
28485　　wîsten si zuo dem altær.
zwâr daz wart dem grâven swær,
wan er ez selb ane sach.
dâ von leit er ungemach
und gedâht in sînem muot:
28490　　ei! herr got der guot,
mîn frou hât der sinn niht
oder der tiufel hât mit ir phliht,
des swüer ich wol einen eit.
er huop sich heim, im was leit.
28495　　dô si daz opfer leit,
ein samît lanc unde wᵉît
si dâ vallen lie.
daz hemdel gie ir ûf diu knie,
daz was von bluot alsô rôt.
28500　　ir frümkeit dô gebôt,
daz si dâ stuont in grôzer scham.
den mantel si wider an sich nam.
zuo der herberg si dô kêrt,
als si ir frümcheit lêrt.
28505　　　　Der grâf kûm des erbeit,
daz si im die wârheit seit.
er sprach: 'sagt mir, frou mîn—
unsinnic mac iur lîp sîn—,
wie habt ir iuch verkêrt
28510　　und iuwern lîp geunêrt?
war zuo sol daz bluotic gewant,
daz man ze kirchen an iu vant?'
dô sagt diu frou die wârheit.
als ez geschach si im daz seit
28515　　und louc im niht als umb ein hâr.
die wârheit seit si im gar.
als der herr daz vernam,
daz si hêt sô grôz scham
erliten durch ir stæticheit,

	She then went to the church,
28480	never forgetting her sense of propriety.
	There she stood with dignity in the church,
	her good breeding crowning her with honor.
	She waited for the offertory,
	and as it was being sung, two trusty knights
28485	led her to the altar.
	This was truly a shock for the Count,
	for he saw it with his own eyes.
	The situation was very uncomfortable for him
	and he thought in his heart,
28490	"Oh, Good Lord God,
	my lady has gone out of her mind,
	or else the Devil has a pact with her,
	I'd swear an oath on it."
	He was so embarrassed that he made off home.
28495	When she had taken the sacrament
	she dropped
	her long, broad, velvet gown.
	The chemise reached only to her knee
	and was bright red with blood.
28500	So great was her courage
	that she stood there despite her great shame.
	She put on her gown again
	and went home
	as her resoluteness demanded.
28505	The Count could hardly contain himself
	until she told him the truth.
	He said, "Tell me, my lady,
	(you must be mad!)
	how could you conduct yourself like this,
28510	dishonoring your own body?
	What is the meaning of this bloody garment
	which you were seen wearing in the church?"
	Then the lady told the truth.
	She told it as it had happened,
28515	concealing not the tiniest detail.
	She told him the whole truth.
	When the lord heard this,
	that she had suffered such great shame
	for the sake of her constancy,

28520 er sprach: 'nû sî dir vor geseit,
 dû bist mir als liep als ê.
 mînem herzen geschach nie sô wê,
 daz ich dich sach blôz stân,
 vil schœniu frou wol getân.'
28525 die froun er zuo im umbevie.
 vil frœlîchen er dô gie
 und sprach: 'liebiu frou mîn,
 alrêrst wil ich dîn eigen sîn.'
 her Fridrîch von dannen reit,
28530 dô er gesach die wârheit,
 dô blôz stuont daz schœn wîp.
 er vorht, ez gieng im an den lîp.

(28533–28662)

 Dar nâch der keiser Fridrîch
 gebôt einen hof rîch.
28535 dâ kômen die fürsten alle hin,
 die tumben und die hêten sin.
 dar fuor ouch sicherlîch
 der herzoc Fridrîch.
 er fuort mit im an sîner schar—
28540 daz ich iu sag für wâr—
 zwei hundert ritter wol getân,
 die fuorten scharlachkappen an:
 die wârn geworht mit flîz;
 dar durch ein edel strich wîz
28545 gie von wîzem scharlach guot.
 des vreut sich dâ der ritter muot.
 niuwe unde schœniu kleit
 fuorten die ritter unverzeit.
 alsô fuoren si gelîch
28550 mit dem fürsten Fridrîch.
 dô der fürst ze hof kam
 und in der keiser vernam,
 dô bat er in vlîziclîch,
 der edel keiser Fridrîch,
28555 daz er æz mit im sîn brôt.
 des bat er sêr und gebôt.
 dô sprach der herzoc Fridrîch:

28520   he said, "Let me say first
         that you are as dear to me as ever.
         My heart was never so troubled
         as when I saw you standing there naked,
         my beautiful, fair lady."
28525   He took the lady in his arms.
         Joyfully he went to her
         and said, "My dear lady,
         from now on I will be in your service."
         Sir Frederick rode away
28530   when he grasped the truth of the matter,
         that the beautiful woman had stood there naked.
         He feared it would cost him his life.

[DUKE FREDERICK OF AUSTRIA]

         After that, the Emperor Frederick
         summoned a great court.
28535   All the princes came,
         the foolish and the wise.
         And of course Duke Frederick [of Austria]
         also made his way there.
         In his retinue
28540   —I tell you the truth—
         he led 200 fine knights,
         who wore caps of scarlet
         skillfully worked;
         a magnificent streak of white
28545   made of white scarlet ran through them.
         This raised the spirits of the knights.[30]
         The brave knights wore
         fine new garments.
         Thus uniformed, they accompanied
28550   Duke Frederick.
         When the Duke reached the court,
         and the Emperor saw him,
         the noble Emperor Frederick
         enthusiastically invited him
28555   to take bread with him.
         This was both an earnest request and a command.
         At this Duke Frederick said:

'daz stüend eim fürsten niht gelîch,
daz ich iur brôt ezzen solt.
28560   war zuo solt dann mîn golt?'
dô sprach der keiser mit sinn:
'Fridrîch, ez wær ein minn
und niht zwâr ein hôchfart.
stüend ez dir übel, ich ez bewart.'
28565   er moht sô vil gebiten niht,
daz er an dem ezzen pfliht
mit im wolt haben ze dheiner zît.
er sprach: 'diu stat ist niht sô wît.
ich verbiut, daz zuo der kuchen dîn,
28570   dhein holz an dem fiur schîn,
daz dir daz nieman veilez geb,
swer mit gemach hie bî mir leb.'
dâ mit er boten sant,
die verbuten zehant,
28575   daz nieman wurd sô stolz,
der dem herzogen holz
gæb umb sîn pfennige;
der müest im entrinnen.
        Do der herzoc moht gehaben niht
28580   holzes, 'daz ist enwiht'
sprach er an der selben stat
zuo sînem schaffær drât,
daz man ein hûs koufe gar,
dâ man die spîs offenbar
28585   solt all bereiten
und die kezzel eiten.
dô des der keiser wart gewar,
zehant sant er boten dar,
daz man im niht mit heile
28590   tæt dhein hûs veile.
dô des der herzoc Fridrîch
wart innen und sîn marschalc rîch,
dô wart er ze râte
des nahtes alsô spâte,
28595   daz er kouft nuzze vil.
daz man im spîs unz an ein zil
bereitet schôn mit sicherheit
bî den nuzzen, als man seit,

"That would little become a Prince,
that I should eat your bread.
28560   Why then do I have gold of my own?"
The Emperor answered him wisely:
"Frederick, it was said in love
and not with impertinence.
If it were to your dishonor, I would have avoided it."
28565   However, he was not able to persuade him
to consent to dine
with him at any time.
He said: "The town is not so large;
I forbid anyone
28570   who lives under my protection
to sell any firewood
to your kitchen."
He at once sent messengers
who announced the prohibition,
28575   that no one should dare
to give the Duke wood,
for all his money;
they were to avoid him.
        When the Duke could not get
28580   wood, he said, "No matter!";
there and then
he told his steward
to buy a house[31]
where all their food
28585   should be prepared openly,
and the cauldrons heated.
When the Emperor learned of this,
he at once sent messengers
that no one could sell him
28590   a house with impunity.
When Duke Frederick and
his powerful marshal learned of this,
he instructed him
late in the night
28595   to buy lots of nuts,
so that his food could be prepared
to his full satisfaction without difficulty,
using the nuts, so it is said,

wann die nuzze schal
28600   glosten alle über al.
daz wart dem keiser kunt getân.
er sprach: 'wâfen, wie ein man
diser ist von Œsterrîch!
jâ wæn ich, im sî niht gelîch.
28605   dâ von erlouben muoz ich im wol,
daz ich für wâr sprechen sol,
wit und swaz er koufen wil,
wan er hât wîses râtes vil.'
         Dar nâch der herzog Fridrîch
28610   reit ze hof sicherlîch.
dô frâgt in der keiser dô,
wer im gerâten hiet iesô
sô mangen frömden list,
der in der stat erzeiget ist.
28615   dô sprach der fürst: 'herre mîn,
mîn rât kan ouch wîse sîn.'
einer schœnen bet er in bat,
den keiser, an der selben stat.
er sprach: 'lieber herre mîn,
28620   möht ez in iuwern hulden sîn,
sô wolt ich iuch des gern biten,
ob ir wært in den siten,
und ob ez iu niht wær ein swær,
daz ir mir zeiget die stechær.'
28625   zehant sprach er: 'des bist gewert.
ist iht des dîn herz gert,
daz sol dir niht sîn verseit.'
die stecher wurden dô bereit,
als er im dô wol gan.
28630   si giengen für irn herren stân.
dô sprach der keiser Fridrîch:
'wîset mir die stecher gelîch
oben ûf disen turn hôch.
die zwên stecher ich hie zôch,'
28635   sprach der keiser Fridrîch.
'dû sihest hiut an in gelîch,
daz si tuont niht wan mîn gebot.
si fürhtent mich mêr danne got.

	for all the nutshells
28600	burned brighter than anything.
	The Emperor was told of this.
	He said: "My, what a man
	is this Lord of Austria!
	I do believe there is no one like him.
28605	So, I have to allow him
	—and indeed I will proclaim it—
	firewood and whatever he wants to buy,
	for he is a very wise man."
	After this, Duke Frederick
28610	rode to court.
	Then the Emperor asked him
	who had taught him
	so many unfamiliar ruses
	which he had demonstrated in the town.
28615	To this the Prince replied "My lord,
	I can have good ideas all by myself!"
	On that same occasion he asked
	a special favor of the Emperor.
	He said: "My dear lord,
28620	if it is your will,
	I would like to ask you
	—if it is your custom
	and if it wouldn't be any trouble—
	to show me the assassins."
28625	At once he said: "This will be granted you.
	If there is anything your heart desires,
	it shall not be denied you."
	The assassins were prepared
	as he had promised him.
28630	They came and stood before their master.
	Then the Emperor Frederick said:
	"Show the assassins up
	to the top of this tall tower for me.
	I raised these two assassins here,"
28635	said the Emperor Frederick;
	"Today you will see that both of them
	will follow my command precisely.
	They fear me more than God.

	ein grôz gebot lâz ich dich sehen,
28640	daz dû mir muost von schulden jehen,
	daz si mich fürhten âne spot
	noch mêr danne got.'
	der turn fünfzic ellen hêt
	an der hœhen dâ er stêt.
28645	dar ûf si stuonden sicherlîch.
	dô sprach der keiser Fridrîch:
	'val her ab, sælic man!'
	zehant er springen began
	ab dem turn daz er zerbrast.
28650	daz was an im ein bœser last.
	den herzogen wundert des sêr.
	er sprach: 'herr, ich gesach nie mêr,
	daz iu ein sô junger man
	wær sô gar undertân.'
28655	dem andern winkt er nider.
	den zuct er bî im hin wider;
	anders hêt er den tôt genomen,
	niht lebentic wær er dannen komen.
	dô sprach herzoc Fridrîch: .
28660	'herr, ich sag iu sicherlîch,
	iu mac dhein fürst vor gestân,
	oder sîn leben muoz zergân.'

(28663–28690)

	Dar nâch stuont ez unlange zît,
	unz in der werlt wît
28665	der keiser wart ze bann getân
	von eim ieglîchen pfeflîchen man;
	die tâten in in den ban dô.
	dar umb gap er niht ein strô.
	der bâbst in ze banne tet
28670	und vil übel von im ret,
	er wær ein ketzerlîcher man,
	dâ von sô wær er in dem ban.
	daz keiseramt wær im entseit.
	dô wart dem herzogen leit,
28675	dem fürsten ûz Œsterrîch.

	I will let you see a great command,
28640	so that you will have to admit
	that—and this is no joke—
	they fear me even more than God.
	The tower was fifty cubits high
	at its highest point;
28645	they were all standing on top of it.
	Then the Emperor Frederick said
	"Fall down, you happy man!"
	At once he leapt from the tower,
	and splattered on the ground.
28650	It was the worst kind of letdown for him.
	The Duke was utterly amazed at this.
	He said, "Lord, I have never seen
	such a young man
	as submissive as he was to you."
28655	He waved the other one down.
	He pulled him back again;
	otherwise he would have died,
	he would not have escaped with his life.
	Then Duke Frederick said,
28660	"Lord, I tell you the truth,
	no prince can stand before you
	or it will cost him his life."

[THE SECOND EXCOMMUNICATION OF FREDERICK II][32]

	After this it was not long
	before the Emperor was placed under the ban
28665	throughout the whole world,
	by every member of the priesthood;
	they excommunicated him.
	He couldn't have cared less.
	The Pope placed him under the ban
28670	and spoke much evil about him,
	that he was a heretic
	and had been excommunicated because of it,
	that he had been deposed from the imperial throne.
	The Duke was saddened by this,
28675	the Prince from Austria.

	dar umb sô fuor er sicherlîch
	gegen Pülln in daz Walhenlant
	und macht si zuo friunt zehant,
	den bâbst und den keiser dâ.
28680	durch sînen willen liezen si ez sâ.
	dô gap der bâbst Gregorius
	dem herzogen ein gâb alsus,
	daz Stîr unde Ôsterlant
	nimmer dhein ban wurd bekant
28685	von dem stuol sicherlîch
	noch dheim bâbst wunniclîch
	in siben jârn, daz ist wâr—
	die hantfest gap er im gar—,
	noch daz sîn liut sicherlîch
28690	nieman verbien in Œsterrîch.
	Nâch Christi geburt zwelif hundert jâr und drîzic jâr daz geschach.

(28691–28848)

	Nû hiet ich vil gar verdagt,
	daz ich iu niht ein mær sagt
	von dem keiser Fridrîch,
	waz er dô tet in sînem rîch,
28695	ein vil wârez mære.
	die Venedigære
	wolden im niht undertân sîn.
	dô hiez er korn unde wîn
	in gemeinclîch verbieten.
28700	dô muosten si sich nieten
	vil hungers in der stat,
	wan si der keiser bat,
	wan si korns niht mohten gewinnen
	dann als vil in mohten bringen
28705	di kiel über des meres fluot.
	niht korns hêt diu stat guot:
	niht anderr spîs fuort man der stat;
	von rœmischer erd nieman bat
	in füeren einen metzen:
28710	des muosten si sich letzen
	beidiu weizen unde korn.
	der keiser ez verbôt mit zorn,
	daz man in fuort dhein korn.

Therefore he made his way
to Apulia in Italy,[33]
and there reconciled them,
the Pope and the Emperor.
28680   For his sake they abandoned their conflict.
Then Pope Gregory
gave the Duke the following gift,
that Styria and Austria
would not be placed under any ban
28685   by the papal see,
nor, happily, by any Pope
for seven years—this is true,
he gave him his guarantee—
nor would any of his people
28690   excommunicate anyone in Austria.
This happened in the year of our Lord 1230.

[THE SIEGE OF VENICE][34]

Now I have quite omitted
to tell you a story
of the Emperor Frederick
and what he did in his empire,
28695   a tale of truth.
The Venetians
did not wish to submit to his authority.
So he ordered that corn and wine
should be completely prohibited to them.
28700   Now they had to suffer
much hunger in the city,
for the Emperor's command meant
that they could procure no corn
except what they could bring
28705   by sea in boats.
The good city had no corn left:
no other provisions were brought to the city;
no one in the Roman world
would send them a single measure of grain,
28710   and so they had to do without
both wheat and corn.
In his fury the Emperor forbade
anyone to deliver corn to them.

daz was in leit unde zorn.
28715   doch kund er niht gemachen
mit dheiner lei sachen
noch mit dheiner swære,
daz im Venedigære
wolden wesen undertân.
28720   si wolden selb ir herren hân.
daz triben si unz an die zît,
daz sich under in huop ein strît.
der strît geschach ûf dem mer.
galîn und barken, was ein her,
28725   fuoren ûf dem mer enzat.
der strît huop sich drât.
doch gelanc dem keiser Fridrîch,
daz die sînen sicherlîch
den sic an gewunnen.
28730   swelich nicht entrunnen,
die viengen si an der zît.
ez was ein herter strît.
si viengen dâ mit swære
sehs Venedigære
28735   und des herzogen sun.
nû wil ich iu kunt tuon,
wie ez den selben dô ergienc,
die man ûf dem mer vienc.
die selben fuorten si gelîch
28740   für den keiser Fridrîch.
an der selben stat
der keiser si bat
füern in einen karkær.
daz wart den gevangen swær,
28745   wan si ungezzen muosten wesen—
des mohten si kûm genesen—
zwâr unz an den dritten tac.
vil ungüetlîch man ir pflac.
dô der dritt tac erschein,
28750   dô hiez der keiser si gemein
füern ûz dem karkære;
diu zît was in niht swære.
zwên tisch er dô rihten hiez.

This was a source of suffering and anger to them.
28715   Yet he could not
by any method
nor by any kind of coercion
force the Venetians
to be subject to him.
28720   They wanted to have their own rulers.
They persisted in this until it reached the point
where war broke out between them.
The battle took place at sea.
Galleys and barques—what an army of them!—
28725   were deployed all over the sea.[35]
The battle blew up suddenly.
However, the Emperor Frederick succeeded
in ensuring that his side
won the victory.
28730   They soon captured
all who did not flee.
It was a cruel battle.
With great difficulty
they captured six Venetians
28735   and the son of the Doge.
Now I will tell you
what happened to these men
who were captured at sea.
They were all alike brought
28740   before the Emperor Frederick.
On the spot
the Emperor ordered them
to be placed in prison.
That was hard on the captives,
28745   for they had to remain without food
—they barely survived it—
for three days.
They were entertained most inhospitably.
When the third day came.
28750   the Emperor had them all
brought from the prison.
They were in no hurry.
He had two tables set up.

an den einen er si liez
28755   sitzen sicherlîche:
dô saz der keiser rîche
an dem andern gegen in.
wiltbræt unde voglîn
truoc man im und spîs genuoc.
28760   ich sag iu waz man in für truoc:
daz ir êrste riht solt sîn:
man gap in niht brôt noch wîn—
daz was den gevangen swær—,
ein schüzzel volle Bernær
28765   sazt man für si zuo einer geschiht.
zwâr daz was ir êrste riht.
daz was in ein grôziu swær.
ein schüzzel vol Venedigær
muost diu ander schüzzel sîn.
28770   diu dritt riht wârn Augustîn.
diu vierd was fîn golt,
wan in der keiser nie wart holt.
diu fünft riht brantez golt was.
edel gestein diu sehst was.
28775   daz was ein grôz nôt.
ûf den tisch leit man für brôt
grôz zelten von silber wîz.
der keiser sprach zuo in mit flîz:
'ezzt, ir herren, die spîs!'
28780   dô sprach der jung und der grîs:
'wir mügen diser spîs niht.
der hunger der hât mit uns pfliht.'
der keiser Fridrîch dô sprach:
'nû wænt ir, herren, ir habt gemach,
28785   wan ir habt golt und edel gestein:
des mügt ir ezzen klein.
daz hân ich hie gesehen.
des müezt ir mir der wârheit jehen.'
dar nâch hiez er in ze ezzen geben
28790   unde nert fürbaz ir leben.
zehant der keiser einen boten drât
sant ze Venedig in die stat,
ob man im wolt die stat geben,
oder die gevangen müesten ir leben
28795   lâzen dâ gelîch.

	He had them sit
28755	at one of these:
	there sat the mighty Emperor
	at the other, facing them.
	Venison and wildfowl
	were laid before him, and food in plenty.
28760	I will tell you what was laid before the prisoners
	as their first course:
	they were given neither bread nor wine
	—that was hard on the captives—
	but a bowl of coins from Verona
28765	was placed before them.
	Truly, that was the first course.
	This was most upsetting for them.
	A bowl of Venetian coins
	was the second dish.
28770	The third course was Augustines.[36]
	The fourth was fine gold,
	for the Emperor was rather displeased with them.
	The fifth course was refined gold.
	Gemstones were the sixth.
28775	This posed a considerable problem for them.
	On the table, instead of bread,
	were laid great cakes of white silver.
	The Emperor urged them
	"Eat your dinner, gentlemen!"
28780	Then young and old declared:
	"We cannot eat this food.
	But we are very hungry."
	Then the Emperor Frederick said:
	"Now gentlemen, you believe you are provided for
28785	because you have gold and jewels;
	but you can't eat a lot of those!
	I've seen that now with my own eyes,
	so you can't deny it."
	After that he ordered them to be fed
28790	and he provided for them in every way.
	Next the Emperor ordered a message
	to be sent to the city of Venice
	that if they did not give him the city
	the prisoners would all
28795	be put to death.

alsô enbôt der keiser rîch.
die Venedigær antwurten sô,
si gæben im niht ein dürrez strô,
ob er si all hienge,
28800 swie halt ez in ergienge.
dô diu botschaft wider kam
und der keiser daz vernam,
dô hiez er mit sachen
ein hôhes antwerc machen
28805 und dar ûf zwên masboum.
des nâmen alle Walch goum,
daz er die masboum zesamen sluoc;
die wurden beide hôch genuoc.
er hiez si ûf daz antwerc tragen.
28810 mit îsen wurden si beslagen
an daz antwerc vest.
ein rinderhût die man west
hiez man zuo einer bulgen machen
an den masboum mit sachen
28815 unde mit seilen lanc,
diu dâ hêten mangen swanc.
swann der wint dar an gienc,
so diu bulg an dem masboum hienc,
sô fluoc si verr von dan.
28820 in die bulg leit man den man,
der des herzogen sun was
von Venedig, als ich ez las.
kæs und brôt man zuo im leit.
an der selben zͤît
28825 kom ein wint daz er strebt.
von der spîs er lenger lebt.
daz antwerc bî des meres fluot
stuont dâ der herr guot
vil hôch an erhangen was.
28830 swer in der stat ze Venedig was,
der sach in varn sicherlîch,
des herzogen sun vil rîch.
des weinet sîn vater sêr,
sîn muoter michels mêr
28835 weint, swann er sich ruorte
und in der wint fuorte.

That was the message from the mighty Emperor.
The Venetians answered
that they couldn't care less
if he hanged them all,
28800 no matter what should happen to them.
When the message came back
and the Emperor heard it,
he ordered a high siege engine
to be built with all due care,
28805 with two masts on top.
All the Italians saw
how he joined the masts together.
They were both very tall.
He had them put on top of the siege engine
28810 and fixed to it firmly
with iron.
A cow hide which they knew of
was made into a leather sack
and expertly attached to the mast
28815 with long ropes,
which could swing freely.
When the wind got up,
where the sack was hanging from the mast,
it flew wildly to and fro.
28820 In the sack they put the man
who was the son of the Doge
of Venice, so I've read.
Cheese and bread were put in with him.
Right away a gust of wind came,
28825 making him wriggle.
He lived longer because he had food.
The siege engine on which
the good man was hanging high
stood by the sea.
28830 Everyone in the city of Venice
must surely have seen him swing,
the son of the mighty Doge.
His father wept bitterly,
his mother even more
28835 when he struggled
and the wind drove him.

alsô lebt er unz er starp.
der keiser dar nâch warp,
daz die sehs sturben dâ
28840   und die gevangen all iesâ.
alsô tôter muost er hangen
an dem masboum und der stangen,
unz daz seil erfûlt gar.
daz sagt uns daz buoch für wâr,
28845   daz in niht half Venediger guot.
er viel in des meres fluot.
daz mer sluoc in an daz lant.
daz wart den Walhen wol bekant.

(28849–28944)

Ze einen zîten daz geschach,
28850   daz der keiser Fridrîch sprach:
'wir süllen bald gâhen,
da wir wizzen valken vâhen.
der hân ich gesehen niht ze vil
mîn tag. dâ von ist ez mîn spil,
28855   daz wir si vâhen; êst an der zît.
ich hân ûz einem hol wît
gesehen valken dar enpfliegen.
dar an mich nieman sol betriegen:
ich sach ir vier oder mêr
28860   fliegen ûz dem hol her.
wær ieman der mir si gewunn,
den wolt ich rîchen und sîn kunn,
swer sich ez törst genemen an.'
doch was bî im dhein man,
28865   dem daz von im möht gezemen,
der die valken wolt nemen.
do sprach under in ein wîser man:
'wer mac sich des genemen an
oder wer möht sîn sô wol gemuot,
28870   daz er umb dhein guot
sînen lîp wolt verliesen?
den mac ich niht erkiesen.'
dô der keiser erhôrt
des wîsen mannes wort,

Thus he lived until he died.
Then the Emperor decreed
that the six should die
28840   and all the prisoners at once.
He [the Doge's son] was to hang dead
from the mast and the crossbar
until the rope rotted.
The book tells us
28845   that all the wealth of Venice didn't help him.
He fell into the sea,
the sea washed him ashore,
and the Italians had to watch it.

[THE FALCON HUNT]

On one occasion it came about
28850   that the Emperor Frederick said
"Let us go quickly to that place
where we know we can catch falcons.
I have never seen so many
in all my days. Therefore it is my pleasure
28855   that we catch them; the time has come.
I have seen falcons there
flying out of a great wide cave.
No one can pull the wool over my eyes:
I saw four of them or more
28860   flying out of the cave.
If anyone can get them for me
I will make him rich, and his family,
whoever dares to undertake this."
But there was no man there
28865   who could get enthusiastic about the challenge
of taking the falcons.
Then a wise man among them said:
"Who can undertake this?
Who could be so courageous
28870   that he would lose his life
for any amount of money?
I can't see such a person."
When the Emperor heard
the wise man's words,

28875 er sprach: 'ich hân mich wol bedâht
und hân ez wol in mîner aht,
daz ich einen man vinden kan,
der sich des tar genemen an.
der müest doch hangen.
28880 umb roup ist er gevangen.'
zehant er nâch dem selben man
sant einen boten dan.
er sprach: 'ich sag dir für wâr,
daz dû muost an dem lîb gar
28885 sterben sicherlîch,'
sô sprach der keiser Fridrîch.
'doch ist dir ditz dinc enteil:
gewinnest dû dar an daz heil,
ich lâz dich genesen.
28890 des solt dû gewis wesen.
ist daz dû wil in disen berc,
würken alsô heldes werc,
daz dû dich lâzest dar in,
und hâst dû dann sölhen sin,
28895 daz dû mir bringst die valken guot,
sô maht dû werden wol gemuot.
ich sag dir, daz selb hol
ist wærlîch allez würm vol.'
dô sprach der nôtig man:
28900 'sît ich muoz daz leben lân,
ob ich iuwern willen niht entæt,
wizzet daz von mir stæt,
ich wil varn in daz hol,
swie ez sî würm alsô vol,
28905 und iu die valken bringen,
swie halt mir sol gelingen.'
'ich sag iu, daz selb luoc
ist an der vinster alsô kluoc,
daz man dâ niht gesehen mac,
28910 swie lieht liuht der tac:
niht wan einer klâfter lanc
hât daz lieht dar în sînn ganc.'
    Zehant wart bereitet dar
seil und schaf, des nam man war,
28915 und lie den jungen man dar in.
zwâr daz was des keisers sin.

28875	he said: "I've thought it over,
	and I have a notion
	that I can find a man
	who would dare to undertake this.
	He is supposed to be hanged.
28880	He's been convicted of robbery."
	Straight away he sent a messenger
	to fetch that same man.
	He said: "I tell you the truth,
	you are certainly going
28885	to be put to death,"
	said the Emperor Frederick,
	"But I will grant you this one chance:
	If you are successful
	I will spare your life.
28890	You have my word on it.
	If you will go into this hill,
	if you are so heroic
	as to go in there,
	and if you are cunning enough
28895	that you bring me these fine falcons,
	then you will be a happy man.
	I tell you frankly, this cave
	is full of serpents."
	At this, the condemned man said:
28900	"Since I must die if
	I do not do as you ask,
	I am determined
	that I will enter the cave
	no matter how many serpents are in it,
28905	and I will bring you those falcons
	by hook or by crook."
	"I tell you, this hole
	is so treacherously dark
	that you can see nothing at all,
28910	no matter how bright the day is.
	the light barely makes it
	two arms' lengths inside."
	At once a rope and a basket
	were prepared where everyone could see it,
28915	and the young man was let into the cave.
	That was precisely the Emperor's idea.

daz sâhen die dâ wâren:
bî vier und zweinzig jâren
was der selb jünglinc:
28920   doch wolt er schaffen sîn dinc:
sîn hâr was swarz sam ein ber;
doch was im zuo dem luog ger
unde wolt dar inne wesen.
daz tet er allez durch genesen.
28925   dô man den jungen man ân schal
lie in den berc ze tal
und er die vinster ersach,
dô leit er grôzen ungemach.
zuo dem nest er dô kêrt,
28930   als in der keiser lêrt,
und nam die jungen valken ab.
daz dûht in ein schœniu hab.
daz seil er dô ruorte,
dann er ez vast fuorte;
28935   dô zôch man in her wider ûz.
dô was er wîzer dann ein strûz,
wan er hêt nindert dhein swarzez hâr:
ez was grâ, daz ist wâr.
daz was im allez geschehen,
28940   des muoz ich von schulden jehen.
die valken er dem keiser bôt.
der liez in dô von sîner nôt
und liez in fürbaz genesen;
dâ von sô muost er vrô wesen.

(28945–28958)

28945   Dar nâch der keiser wart verholn,
den kristen allen vor verstoln,
wan nieman west diu mære
wa er hin komen wære.
ob er wær tôt an der zît,
28950   dâ von ist wærlîch noch ein strît
in welhischen landen über al.
die einen jehent mit grôzem schal,
daz er sî erstorben
und in ein grap verborgen,

Everyone who was there saw it:
that young man
was twenty-four years old,
28920   but he was determined to do what he had to:
his hair was black like a bear's;
yet he was keen to get to the hole
and wanted to be inside.
He did all that to save himself.
28925   When the young man was silently
let down into the hill
and he saw the darkness,
he was terrified.
He made his way to the nest
28930   as the Emperor had instructed him,
and took out the young falcons.
He thought this a fine prize.
He reached for the rope
and gave it a sharp tug;
28935   at this they pulled him out again.
Now he was whiter than an ostrich,
for he had no black hair anywhere:
it was grey, and that's a fact.
All this had happened to him,
28940   I cannot tell a lie.
He gave the Emperor the falcons.
The Emperor pardoned him
and spared his life;
he was very happy about this.

[THE ONCE AND FUTURE KING]

28945   After this, the Emperor disappeared,
hidden from the eyes of all the Christians,
for no one knew
where he had gone.
Whether he died at that time
28950   is still a matter of contention
throughout Italy.
Some proclaim loudly
that he is dead
and hidden in a grave,

28955 sô habent sümlîch disen strît,
       er leb noch in der werlt wît.
       welhez under den beiden sî,
       des mæres bin ich worden frî.

28955   but others hold the opinion
        that he is still at large in the world.
        Which of the two is correct?
        I'm sure I have no idea!

NOTES

WELTCHRONIK, Rudolf von Ems

1.   Refers to the flood. The same word *slac* is used for the plagues of Egypt.

2.   *Wârheit* can be "truth" in an abstract sense (as in 181 below), or "true and trustworthy account" (182, 188); hence it also comes to mean the authoritative source. Here in 132 it refers to Peter Comestor's *Historia scholastica*. In 1568, the *schrift der wârheit* is Honorius Augustodunensis, *Imago mundi*. In 146 and 250, *Gotes wârheit* means the Bible, but in 183 the Bible is the *heilige schrift* precisely to contrast it with the *buoh der wârheit* (182), the non-Biblical sources.

3.   On the Adam and Eve stories, see introduction (p. 9). A good survey of the Adam legends is Brian Murdoch's *Adam's Grace*; Hans Martin von Erffa's *Ikonologie der Genesis* is a useful reference work on Biblical motifs.

4.   This could mean simply that the devil turned his thoughts (*rât*) to the question, but there was a tradition of an infernal council (also *rât*) in which the devil sought counsel (*rât* again) from his peers on the best strategy for tempting Eve.

5.   On the monstrous races, see introduction (pp. 10–11) and the book by John Block Friedman. P. D. A. Harvey's book on the *Mappa Mundi* shows how these fitted into medieval concepts of geography.

6.   See n. 8.

7.   Honorius's punch-line, which Rudolf omits, is that pepper has its black color from this fire.

8.   1524 ff.: The Macrobii are more commonly called Pandae; here their size is highlighted as a counterpoint to the Pygmies, but elsewhere they are known for their long ears, extra fingers and toes, and the peculiarity of being born grey-haired (cf. 1590 ff.). Griffins are a monstrous hybrid of lion and eagle. A *klafter* (fathom) was the length of both outstretched arms, roughly two meters (six feet). This should properly be contrasted with *dûmelle* (cubit), the distance from the elbow to the tip of the

thumb, roughly 50 centimetres (20 inches) which Rudolf used some twenty lines earlier (1505). However, in the chronicles, *dûmelle* and *klafter* seem often to be used interchangeably. Honorius has *cubitum* here, the same word he used of the Pygmies (Rudolf's 1505). See also note 28 on Enikel 28357.

9.   1547 ff.: The Anthropophagi (man-eaters) are simply cannibals in Pliny, but become specifically parent-eaters in the later Latin tradition.

10.   1562 ff.: The raw-fish-eaters are sometimes called Ichtyophagi.

11.   1573 ff.: Various different fantastic races had reversed feet, most notably the Antipodes.

12.   1583 ff.: The people with dogs' heads may be called Cynocephales.

13.   1615 ff.: Rudolf has translated *Monoculus* (one-eyed) with *Einstern* (one-star), for Latin *oculi* could refer poetically to the stars. In this tradition, Monoculi and Arimaspi are alternative names for the Homeric Cyclopes (singular Cyclops!), though in Roman times there really was a Scythian people called the Arimaspians. The Ceno-pods are more usually called Sciopods. Pliny calls them Monocoli (one-legged), which resulted in a confusion with the Monoculi; hence the two appear together here.

14.   1637 ff.: The headless people are called Blemmiae.

15.   1652 ff.: The apple smellers are sometimes called Astomi (mouthless), as they do not eat, though in medieval manuscript illustrations they do have mouths, which presumably they need for speaking.

16.   *Zenocrota*—Honorius has *ceucocrota*.

17.   The yale is called *eale* in Honorius's Latin, and in the German text the *e* has been misread as a *c*. Though the best manuscript has *cale*, other normally less reliable ones do have *eale*, so the mistake may not be Rudolf's. This is an ancient name for an Ethiopian animal, perhaps the rhinoceros or a kind of buffalo. In the Middle Ages it becomes a fantastic beast popular in heraldry, in the French and English traditions often called centicore.

CHRISTHERRE-CHRONIK

1.   At the beginning of the excerpt, Jacob is fleeing northwards from the Judean desert, to escape the vengeance of his brother, Esau. Though the immediate source is Peter Comestor's *Historia scholastica*, the Old Testament stories in this chronicle follow the Bible very closely. This theophany (vision of God) comes from Gen. 28.10 ff. The geography is slightly confused (7904); rather, he went northwards from Beersheba (in the Judean desert, just south of Jerusalem) to Haran, in the region of Paddan Aram, which straddles what is now northern Syria and southern Turkey, around the sources of the Euphrates. Medieval writers often had only a vague notion of Biblical geography. Kiriath-Jearim (Latin: *Cariathiarim*) is an important town in

later Old Testament history, but does not appear in Genesis. The idea of Jacob avoiding the Canaanites comes from the Comestor. Luz is the old name for Bethel (Gen. 28.19), a little north of Jerusalem.

2.   7951 ff.: This commenting insert into the Bible's narrative is from the Comestor. Highlighting the prophetic significance of Old Testament events is standard Christian narrative practice going back to the New Testament (e.g., Matt. 1.22 f.).

3.   7953–57: See Figure 2 (p. 15) for these lines as they appear in a late fourteenth-century manuscript. Note the diphthongization (*sein* for *sin*, etc.) which set in in the later thirteenth century. Note also the variant reading of line 7955, and the general fluidity of spelling and syntax.

4.   8000 ff.: This promise is not in Gen. 28, but Jacob's return to Bethel is recorded in Gen. 35; there he built an altar, not a city. Note that *stat* originally means "place," but comes also to mean "town" from the twelfth century onwards. (Modern German distinguishes the spellings *Statt* and *Stadt*.) Both meanings are to be found in this passage, where the Comestor has first *locus* (7981), then *urbs* (8001). Bethel means "House of God"; cf. 7983 and 8007.

5.   Laban speaking. But the punctuation, as always, is that of the modern editor. If we remove two inverted commas, this line could as easily be spoken by Jacob.

6.   Exceptionally, *libe* is a variant of *liebe* (cf. *dinen/dienen* in 8055 and 8060), and not a plural of *lip*.

7.   8073 f.: A rhetorical motif from love poetry which has a certain irony, since Jacob will have to do precisely this.

8.   In the Bible, Jacob marries Rachel a week after marrying Leah, and must then work seven years for her, but many retellings make him wait till the end of the seven years before they can marry.

9.   *lieben* is an impersonal verb, like Modern German *gefallen*; *di libt im* = he loves her.

10.   8231 ff.: On the *incidentia*, see the introduction (p. 16). Achaea is an area of Greece, but often refers to the whole Greek world. Eleusis was an important town about 20 km north-west of Athens. *Irmonis* is a misreading; the Latin sources have *Lacus Tritonis*.

11.   For *und* read *under*.

12.   Minerva was the Roman goddess of crafts and trade guilds, often equated with the Greek deity Pallas Athene. Here she is credited with inventing spinning. Elsewhere, for example in the chronicles of Rudolf and Enikel, this accolade is given to Adam's daughter Noema.

13.   The mandrake was said to be an aphrodisiac and to induce pregnancy. The ultimate source is Gen. 30.14 f. Rachel has Jacob's attention, but remains barren, whereas Leah is fertile but her husband will not sleep with her. The deal is intended to give both sisters a child.

WELTCHRONIK, JANS ENIKEL

1.   Job is one of the most popular Old Testament figures in medieval culture. In early German literature, he is especially important for an understanding of Hartmann's *Armer Heinrich* and Tepl's *Ackerman*, but there are references and allusions to him in many of the major works. For theologians he was important for reflections on the problem of pain, and Pope Gregory the Great wrote a very influential book on him. Ordinary people knew him especially through the words of the funeral mass. Lawrence Bessermann's book surveys this tradition. On Enikel's version, see the discussion in my introduction (p. 19).

2.   But see 13384 (and 13454).

3.   13279–330: See Figure 3 (p. 20) for these lines as they appear in an early fifteenth-century manuscript. Note textual variants, such as *gnaden* for *gâb* in 13280 or the omission of *freud* in 13281. These variants can be followed in Strauch's apparatus (pp. 251–52 of the critical edition), where this manuscript is referred to by the siglum *14*.

4.   13322, 4: Job was an unofficial patron saint of lepers, and is named in the Old High German charms against worms.

5.   Numerical exaggeration is a feature of Enikel's narratives. Cf. Job 1.2 and 42.12.

6.   That is, whether it was God or the devil who gave them the papacy; cf. 22396.

7.   The myth of Pope Joan appears here for the first time in the German language. See Alain Boureau's book on the development of the myth.

8.   Pope Sylvester II, born Gerbert of Aurillac (ca. 940–1003). See my introduction (p. 19). The origins of this scurrilous tale about a man who was actually an able and learned pope are discussed in the essay by Karl Schulteß.

9.   *vlætic* means "beautiful, delicate"; here it has an emphatic function.

10. Because, quite simply, that is where one conjures up a devil.

11. The man could be naked here as part of his ritual, though it sounds odd in 22439 and 22449, where the bishop is dictating a letter to him. But a succession of clothes is a feature of this story, and nakedness is often a sensationalizing element of Enikel's storytelling, so probably we are to understand this literally. Otherwise, read *nackent* as "penniless."

12. *Santa Croce in Gerusalemme* (the Church of the Holy Rood in Jerusalem) is situated only a short distance from the Lateran, which at that time was the residence of the Popes. The original name of this church was simply *Hierusalem*, as the floor was packed with soil from the Holy Land.

13. Ypres in West Flanders (Belgium) was famous for textiles.

14. *Milte* is one of the courtly virtues characterizing the ideal ruler, here pursued to the point of absurdity.

15. 26639, 58: Here, "heathen" means "Muslim." The assumption that Muslims saw Mohammed as God was natural given the status of Jesus in Christianity. The same word "heathen" is used for the ancient religions, and the two merge into a single blurred conception of the non-Christian world. Elsewhere Enikel makes Mohammed one of the gods of the ancient Philistines, while other medieval texts regularly present Islam as polytheistic. This is probably due to ignorance rather than mischief.

16. This is now historical reporting, though it does still frequently have the quality of a tale. See the comments in the introduction (p. 21) on Enikel's presentation of Frederick II, and for the historical background see the biography by David Abulafia. The excommunication in this passage took place in 1227.

17. 28023–24 : Or: "pillage and arson arose because of that one land," depending on whether *daz selb lant* refers back to 28011 or 28018.

18. 28074 ff.: The following section, and also that after 28078, is missing from the main manuscripts, but is probably genuine. It survives in MS 10, a fifteenth-century paper manuscript now in Berlin.

19. 28074.29 f.: The text has *vor Holde*, which is awkward. Strauch, who edited Enikel in 1891, emends to *frou*: the reference is then to Frau Hulda, the Germanic goddess, familiar also in the folklore of the Christian Middle Ages: the arrival of her cohort is typically accompanied by loud noise.

20. The text has *paid* (= *beide*), which makes little sense here; *waid* is Strauch's proposed emendation.

21. Every so often Enikel adds such a phrase which may or may not indicate that he is working with a written source, but at any rate lends authority to the account; cf. 28164. Here it falls in the middle of the Emperor's speech, which in an unpunctuated text gives the impression that the emperor speaks these words. In a footnote in the edition, Strauch comments acidly, "Der gedankenlose reimer legt hier die bekannte formel Friedrich II in den mund!!" But Strauch is frequently too disparaging about Enikel. A person telling a story or joke might well interrupt direct speech to make an aside to the audience. Enikel's informality might simply reflect the fact that his text was to be read aloud.

22. *Bern* and *Verona* are variant forms of the same name, and in medieval texts both can refer to either modern Bern (in Switzerland) or Verona (Italy), or indeed to Bonn. But the Italian "Bern" is most likely here given the origins of this story (see 28172) and Enikel's usage elsewhere. In the case of the coin in 28774, the reference is definitely Verona.

23. *Walch* is "Italian" or "Frenchman." We may sense here a whiff of ethnic sneering. Other Middle High German writers also display anti-Italian sentiment, most famously Walther von der Vogelweide 34.5.

24. This tale is based on a short Old French fabliau by Jacques de Baisieux which in style comes close to the courtly novel. The insertion of this kind of writing into the historical account is typical of Enikel. We find a similar mixing of genres in the

Kaiserchronik, though the intention there is more pious. On this story, see Dunphy, "Ritter mit dem Hemd." This Friedrich von Antfurt is fictional, though the name may have been borrowed from a real person who lived in the twelfth century.

25. The text has *ane*, which might translate "and I would not be without pain." This is illogical, and the Leipzig manuscript MS 9 (fifteenth century, paper), which often has good readings, has *und ich doch möcht unschuldig sein*, indicating perhaps that the medieval readers were also unsure what to make of the line. Strauch's emendation to *arne* (= *ernten*, often used metaphorically with punishment) seems to solve the problem.

26. Metaphorical reference to the splinters of a lance which might injure a knight while jousting. Echoes of Luke 2.35 (referring to the Virgin Mary: "Yes, a sword shall pierce through thy own soul also")?

27. 28260, 63: *meinen* is either "to mean" or "to love" (common idea: "to fix one's thoughts on something").

28. *elle* is synonymous with *dûmelle* (cf. note 8 on Rudolf 1524 ff.). In a Biblical context we tend to translate it with "cubit."

29. 28441, 47: *Stefanstag zu Pfingsten* is the Monday after Pentecost.

30. This line is incomplete in the main text of the *Weltchronik*, but we can borrow the text from the parallel passage in *Fürstenbuch* 2480, which is confirmed by MS 9.

31. Presumably the idea is to strip the house of its timbers.

32. This is the excommunication of 1245, but some of the details here, including the date and the name of the pope, and the involvement of the Austrian duke (Leopold, not Frederick) relate to the events of 1227–30. On the other hand, line 28673 does refer to 1245; Popes claimed the right to depose emperors, but Innocent IV was the first to attempt to do so. See introduction (p. 22).

33. Thus MS 9. The main manuscripts have *Ôsterlant*, but this makes no sense: Duke Frederick is coming from Austria, and Apulia is in Southern Italy.

34. 28691 ff.: Frederick never besieged Venice, but he did impose a corn embargo, and he did on a different occasion hang the son of the Doge. A sea battle between Venetian and Imperial forces is also recorded.

35. *enzat varn* (from *enzetten*) is "to be scattered." Here meaning either "deployed" or "routed."

36. Imperial coins; all emperors could be referred to as Caesar Augustus. In his life of Constantine, Enikel makes a remark which links these with the original Emperor Augustus (25164 f.).

Medieval Institute Publications is a program
of The Medieval Institute, College of Arts
and Sciences, Western Michigan University

Typeset in 10/12 New Baskerville
with New Baskerville display
Designed by Linda K. Judy
Composed by Julie Scrivener
at Medieval Institute Publications
Manufactured by Cushing-Malloy, Inc.—Ann Arbor, Michigan

Medieval Institute Publications
College of Arts and Sciences
Western Michigan University
1903 W. Michigan Avenue
Kalamazoo, Michigan 49008-5432
www.wmich.edu/medieval/mip/

WESTERN MICHIGAN UNIVERSITY